Reflections on the Gospel of John

Reflections on the Gospel of John

JOHANNES LAUTEN

Floris Books

Translated by Cynthia Hindes

Originally published in German as *ER muss wachsen: Erfahrungen im Johannes-Evangelium* by Alcorde Verlag, Essen

First published in English in 2022 by Floris Books
© 2012 Johannes Lauten
This English edition © 2022 Floris Books

All rights reserved. No part of this book may be reproduced in any form without written permission of Floris Books, Edinburgh
www.florisbooks.co.uk

British Library CIP Data available
ISBN 978-178250-791-8
Printed in Great Britain by CPI Group (UK) Ltd, Croydon

 Also available as an eBook

 Floris Books supports sustainable forest management by printing this book on materials made from wood that comes from responsible sources and reclaimed material

Contents

Foreword   7

1. Who is the Writer of John's Gospel?   11
2. The Disciple Whom the Lord Loved   18
3. Encounters with Christ   25
4. God's Questions for Human Beings   37
5. The Secret of the Centre   44
6. The Tidings of Becoming   50
7. Not Yet   55
8. The Working of Grace   64
9. Becoming the Son of Man   70
10. I Am   80
11. Jesus Christ's Path to the Cross   94
12. An Easter Path   103
13. Christ, the Coming One   109
14. Remain in Me and I in You   119
15. The Human Being: God's Dwelling   125
16. Knowledge and Faith   132

Bibliography   141

Foreword

The Gospel of John as the Gospel of the Logos, the creative Word of the world, has a special place in the canon of the four gospels. In many respects, it is not only particularly precise in its description of earthly conditions and historical details, but in its condensation of the events of the life and work of Jesus Christ and through the fullness of his words and speeches, it is the direct revelation of the central figure of our faith, Christ Jesus.

The Greek language, in which the text was originally written, allowed the writer's spiritual intention to be expressed in a very differentiated way. Many frequently used words have a wide range of meanings. Even if the text often appears simple in its form, individual words always require special attention because of their complexity. Thus, for example, the word *doxa* can be translated as idea, opinion, expectation, fantasy, delusion, decision, theorem, reputation, honour, fame, dream image, or even revelation.

Every translation from Greek into a modern language is tantamount to an interpretation, a risk that every translator must face.

The Logos, the spiritual content of the world, became human and in that human being became a spoken word that was audible and could be fixed in writing. This was the first 'translation'. The goal of every translation must be to make Christ Jesus, the Logos, a living, creative and present being.

The reflections presented here are not intended as a commentary, but rather describe paths that can be followed if one pursues motifs or questions in the Gospel of John. They can inspire readers to explore the diverse landscape of that gospel and to follow their own paths of research, of which there are certainly many more.

The author's intention is to try to allow readers to find an inner confirmation of the closeness of Christ and his work of salvation, and to experience the significance of a contemporary Christianity.

Johannes Lauten

The biblical quotations are the author's own translations from the original Greek texts.

1
Who is the Writer of John's Gospel?

Among the four gospels included in the New Testament, the Gospel of John occupies a special place. Questioning where and when it was written and the author's identity began at the end of the second century, soon after its creation. These questions continue today. Excavations carried out in the Basilica of St John in Ephesus in the 1960s unearthed a metal holder containing scrolls that seemed to contain the text of the Gospel of John. The scrolls are said to date from the first or the second century, that is, from the time when Polycarp of Ephesus attests to the presence of John the Presbyter. The writer of John's Gospel is nowhere mentioned by name. The identity of John the Presbyter and his relationship to the writer of the Gospel of John remains a riddle. Today's research believes that it is the son of Zebedee, John, the brother of James. This idea goes back to Irenaeus of Lyon, who died around AD 202.

Without question, the writer is an eyewitness to the life and work of Jesus Christ and the events at Golgotha. In the Crucifixion account, we read how one of the soldiers who was sent to break the legs of the crucified to hasten their death, pierced the side of the already dead Jesus Christ with his lance, 'and immediately blood and water came out.' Then the text continues, 'He who bore witness to these things has himself seen it, and his testimony is true, and he knows that he speaks the truth, so that you too may gain peace of mind' (Jn 19:35). In the last verses of John's Gospel, this eyewitness is mentioned once again as its author. The account of the meeting of the Risen One with the disciples at the morning meal by the Sea of Galilee, and the conversation with Peter about his task and that of the 'disciple whom Jesus loved', precede the last verse. It says of him, 'This is the disciple who wrote all this down and who vouches for it, and we know that his testimony is the truth' (Jn 21:24).

This particular disciple, 'whom Jesus loved', is mentioned late in the text: only in the report of the Last Supper (Jn 13:23–25) do we hear about him. 'One of his disciples who sat at table with him had his head at his bosom; he was the disciple whom Jesus loved. To him, Peter gave a sign that he might find out of whom he was speaking. Then he laid his head on Jesus' breast and said, "Lord, who is it?"'

In John's Gospel, the word *agapan,* love (not in the body-soul sense but understood spiritually) appears often. But rarely does it characterise Christ Jesus' relationship to a human being. In Chapter 11, his love for Mary, Martha, and Lazarus, is mentioned (Jn 11:5). When Lazarus falls ill, his sisters send Jesus a message: 'Lord, the one you love, [*phileis*] is ill' (Jn 11:3). And his love is spoken of for the third time when he weeps in front of his friend's

1. WHO IS THE WRITER OF JOHN'S GOSPEL?

closed tomb. The people who were there in great numbers said, 'See how deeply he loved [*ephilei*] him' (Jn 11:36).

It is unique in all the gospels that a personal relationship of Christ Jesus with someone is emphasised and stressed in this way. Only in the Gospel of Mark is the encounter of Jesus with a nameless person, the rich young man mentioned in the three synoptic gospels, described with the word *agapan*.

> As Jesus continued on his way, a man ran to him, knelt before him and asked him, 'Good Teacher, what must I do to be worthy of deathless life?'
> Jesus answered, 'Why do you call me good? No one is good, but the One and Only God. You know the commandments. Do not kill, do not violate faithfulness, do not steal, slander, or cheat anyone, honour your father and mother.'
> He said to him, 'Teacher, I have observed all these things since my youth.'
> Then Jesus looked into his heart and loved him, saying, 'Then there is only one thing missing. Go, sell all your possessions, and give the proceeds to the poor, and you will acquire a treasure in the spiritual worlds. And then come and accompany me.'
> At these words, the man's eyes darkened, and he left saddened, for he had great riches (Mk 10:17–22).

The question arises whether these two passages

(Jn 11 and Mk 10) can be seen as relating to each other. Is the rich young man of the synoptic gospels, of whom it says in the Gospel of Luke (18:18–24) that he belonged to the upper class of the people, to the ruling (priestly?) dynasty, identical with Lazarus? The formulation *agapan* used for both would speak for it. Is the further conclusion admissible that the writer of John's Gospel, for whom it is also valid, is the same person as Lazarus, whom the Lord loved, whom he called forth from death in Bethany forty days before his death on the cross at Golgotha (Jn 11), and who from then on is inseparably at his side? Is it he who at the Last Supper lies at his breast, who is the only one of Christ's inner circle who stands under the cross? (Jn 19:25–27) Is it he who, along with Peter, hurries to the tomb on Easter morning? (Jn 20:2–10) If so, then the one whom the Lord loved would be the thirteenth in the circle of the twelve disciples. Many things speak for it. Some representations of the Last Supper have thirteen figures. (for example Albrecht Dürer's *The Last Supper*, woodcut from the Great Passion, 1510). Rudolf Steiner also concludes that Lazarus is the beloved disciple, who wrote the Gospel of John.*

The other answer to the John question, familiar since Irenaeus, is that the beloved is the brother of James, the son of Zebedee (see, for instance, Ratzinger).

This can also be justified. James Zebedee is one of the three disciples, Peter, James and John, who are often summoned on special occasions and

---

* Steiner, *The Gospel of St John*, lecture of May 22, 1908.

1. WHO IS THE WRITER OF JOHN'S GOSPEL?

mentioned by name. He is named at the healing of Peter's mother-in-law (Mk 1:29), the raising of Jairus's daughter (Mk 5:37), the transfiguration (Mk 9:2), during the preparation of the Upper Room (Lk 22:8) and at Gethsemane (Mk 14:33). Both brothers are also among the first disciples chosen by Jesus Christ.

But some events make it difficult to see John the son of Zebedee as the one whom the Lord loved. The evangelist Mark tells of a conversation that the disciples had with their Master in Galilee, in which John says, 'We met a man who cast out demons in your name, and we stopped him because he went his own way and not with us.' But Christ rejects him with the words, 'Do not disturb him. No one who acts in my name can easily deny me. Someone who is not against us is for us' (Mk 9:38–40).

Similarly, the evangelist Luke describes an event on the road to Jerusalem.

> And it happened when his days were fulfilled, and he was about to be taken up into heaven, he turned his face to the path to Jerusalem and sent messengers ahead, who along their way came to a Samaritan village to prepare a shelter for him. But he was not received, because his gaze was turned towards the way to Jerusalem. When his disciples James and John saw this, they said, 'Lord, do you want our word to bring fire to fall from heaven for their destruction?' But he turned to them with great severity, 'You

do not know which spirit is giving you this inspiration. The Son of Man did not come to destroy the souls of men, but to save them.' (Lk 9:51–56)

It can strike us as even more curious when we hear of the two brothers James and John

And James and John, the sons of Zebedee, come to Jesus and say, 'Teacher, we would like you to grant us what we ask of you.'
He said to them, 'What do you want me to do for you?'
They said to him, 'Grant us that we may sit beside you in the radiance of your revelation, one on the right hand and the other on the left.'
Jesus replied, '... Can you receive the baptism by which I am baptised?'
They said, 'We can.'
Then Jesus said to them, 'You also shall empty the cup that I drink, and you shall receive the baptism with which I am baptised. But to give away the places on my right or left is not in my power. Those for whom they are destined will sit there.' (Mk 10:35–40)

Could this John, of whom the evangelists report in such a way, be the one whom the Lord loved?
Who, then, is the writer? If it is John the son of Zebedee, then he is one of the most intimate and first disciples of Jesus, an eyewitness of Jesus' life from the days immediately after the Jordan baptism until his death.

1. WHO IS THE WRITER OF JOHN'S GOSPEL?

☙

In his fundamental work on the question of John, Martin Hengel explains in detail the conclusion of contemporary theological research.

> Not only the [John's] Epistles and the Apocalypse but also – since its spreading through the church by John the Ephesian – the Gospel are connected. Of course, this is not the Zebedean and apostle ... but that mysterious figure who, though not a member of the circle of twelve ... bore the honorary name, *the Lord's disciple.* (p. 205).

Hengel says in summary, 'A Zebedean formulation, the dominant view from the middle of the second century ... has too many historical reasons against it to be upheld in good conscience' (p. 318).

Lazarus became a disciple through his resurrection and was already deeply connected to Christ Jesus before that. He was the one closest to him during the three holy days from Maundy Thursday evening to Easter Sunday evening. If the beloved is Lazarus, then he received the name John only through the close relationship of the five Johannine writings in the New Testament in terms of content and style, because only in the Apocalypse (1:4; 1:9; 22:8) does the name John appear as the writer of the text.

The answer to the question, who the writer of the Gospel of John is, may continue to remain a mystery.

2

The Disciple Whom the Lord Loved

This disciple's destiny is mystifying, even though its culmination, an illness leading to death, is extensively described in the eleventh chapter, the central chapter of John's Gospel.

His raising from death leads to the Sanhedrin's decision to kill both Jesus and Lazarus.

> Then the chief priests and the Pharisees called the Sanhedrin together and said, 'This man performs many signs. If we let him continue to do this, all will believe in him, and the Romans will come and take this holy place and people from us.' (Jn 11:47f)

And a few days later, when Jesus is again with Lazarus in Bethany, it is said,

> Many of the Jews found out that Jesus was in Bethany, but they came not only for his sake but also because they wanted to see Lazarus, whom he had raised from the dead. The high priests, however, discussed how they could kill Lazarus as well, for, through him, many believed in Jesus. (Jn 12:9–11)

2. THE DISCIPLE WHOM THE LORD LOVED

John's Gospel does not speak much of this disciple whom the Lord loved except in the eleventh chapter. Jacobus de Varagine's Golden Legend (Legenda Aurea) describes the three siblings Mary, Martha, and Lazarus as very rich, which could lead to the assumption that Lazarus is the same figure that the evangelist Luke calls one of the 'rulers' (Lk 18:18) and of which the evangelist Mark says that Jesus loved him (Mk 10:21).

About this man's encounter with Christ Jesus, the synoptic gospels report that Jesus advised him to separate himself from all his riches, to give the proceeds to the needy and then give his life a new direction (Mt 19:16–22; Mk 10:17–22; Lk 18:18–23). The gospel reports that Christ Jesus invites him to

> 'Come and accompany me.' At these words
> ... he left saddened, for he had great riches.
> (Mk 10:21f).

Could he be the one of whom John's Gospel writes in Chapter 11? This could only be substantiated by the words 'Jesus loved', since they are only used in the gospels about certain persons, for Lazarus and his sisters (Jn 11:3, 5 and 35), the 'rich young man' (Mk 10:21), and the unnamed 'other disciple' (Jn 19:26; 20:2; 21:7; 21:20).

The placement of the reports about the rich young man and the raising of Lazarus makes it clear that these events must have happened near the beginning of Holy Week so that this positioning in the text also expresses the close connection of the Lord's beloved with the central events of the Passion.

At the end of Jesus' encounter with the rich young man, the gospel says that he went his way full of sorrow. After the raising of Lazarus, we hear Christ Jesus say, 'Unbind him and let him go' (Jn 11:44). And the one whom the Lord loved walked his path and remained close to the Master until his death on the cross.

What happened to him between the rich young man's question and the raising of Lazarus? The description raises questions.

Why did Jesus wait so long with his disciples before going to Bethany?

How was Lazarus dead?

Why the agitation in the Sanhedrin?

News of the illness of the one he loved reached the Lord at Bethany on the eastern bank of the Jordan, where John had baptised earlier. Jesus had gone with his disciples across the Jordan to the place of his baptism and stayed there (Jn 10:40). The two Bethanys (on the Mount of Olives and the Jordan) are about 14 kilometres (8 miles) in a straight line and are connected by the Wadi Qelt, the ancient steep footpath from Jericho to Jerusalem. Walking, it is still a hard day's march.

The two sisters Mary and Martha, send a message to him that their brother is *asthenēs* – ill, laid low. The Greek word denotes inner weakness and powerlessness, in contrast to *nosos*, a disease sent by the gods. What caused it? If one considers the heavy burden this person was to bear in the coming days and weeks up to Golgotha and beyond, then it cannot have been a constitutional weakness.

2. THE DISCIPLE WHOM THE LORD LOVED

Jesus' answer to the sisters' message is puzzling. 'This illness does not lead to death, but to the glory of God, so that through it, the Son of God may be glorified' (Jn 11:4). Why this distinction between the glory of God and the glory of the Son of God? Jesus himself seems to attach importance to them when we hear him say in the temple, 'Up to now, the Father has been at work; from now on, I too am at work' (Jn 5:17). Is the direction of work different? The Father works from outside. 'I did not come down from heaven to live according to my will, but to complete the will of the One who sent me' (Jn 6:38). Christ works from within. He will dwell in human beings and work in them.

> Remain faithful in me, and I will remain in you ... I am the vine; you are the branches. Anyone who keeps my being in them, in them will I work, and they will bring forth abundant fruit of the spirit, for, without me, you can do nothing. (Jn 15:4f)

If Lazarus were the rich young man, did he enter his path of destiny by asking, 'What should I do?' (Mk 10:17) Was he acting from the I, that is, from the power of the One whose name is I AM the I AM?

After the disposal of all his wealth, a tremendous weakness takes possession of him. The riches of which three evangelists speak must have been not only material. If the rich young man, as ruler (*archōn*, Lk 18:18), belonged to the ruling caste of priests, then spiritual goods, holy knowledge of the temple, were also his own, which, after the encounter with

Christ Jesus, were to be transformed and given further to the ignorant, the poor in spirit.

After the news, Jesus stayed two more days with his disciples in Bethany on the other side of the Jordan (Jn 11:6). Then, after three days had passed, he went with his disciples to Bethany on the Mount of Olives, the home of the three siblings – Mary, Martha and Lazarus – and we hear him say to his disciples, 'Lazarus, our friend, is sleeping, but I will go and wake him up from sleep' (Jn 11:11).

He allows three days to pass before he awakens his friend Lazarus from death. Three days is the period that must be completed from the Last Supper to the completion of the resurrection on Easter evening. The same period appears in the pre-Christian initiation rites of the mysteries. And three days is not only important here in the life of Jesus. Luke the evangelist says of the twelve-year-old Jesus, 'And it came to pass that after three days they [the parents] found him in the holy place; he sat in the presence of the teachers, listened to them and put his questions to them' (Lk 2:46).

To his disciples, Christ Jesus emphasises the fact that Lazarus died, and he speaks of his 'joy for your sake that I was not there so that your faith might grow' (Jn 11:14).

At the beginning of the story, the gospel says that the friend was suffering an illness that was to lead to the revelation of the Son of God (Jn 11:4). Christ Jesus later says that he would perform an awakening from sleep (of death) so that the disciples' faith would be strengthened (Jn 11:15). And now, in conversation with the sister Martha in Bethany,

2. THE DISCIPLE WHOM THE LORD LOVED

after Lazarus is already in his grave for four days, we hear the Lord say, 'Your brother will rise again' (Jn 11:23).

He does not say, I will raise him, but Lazarus himself will rise. The power of love that flows from Christ to the friend in need becomes in him the power of resurrection and new life. 'I am the resurrection and the life. Anyone who finds confidence in me will find life in death, and every living person who believes in me will not suffer the second death for all time' (Jn 11:25f). This resurrection of the beloved friend then takes place in several steps.

Deeply aroused, Christ Jesus asks the crowd that has assembled, 'Where did you bury him?' (Jn 11:34). We feel reminded of the Lord's question to Adam in the account of creation, 'Where are you?' (Gn 3:9). God has lost the human being a second time; Adam under the trees, Lazarus under the stones.

And again, a deep convulsion seizes Christ Jesus when he comes to the closed rocky cave and says, 'Roll aside the stone' (Jn 11:39).

> Then he raised his eyes and prayed, 'Father, I thank you for having heard me. I knew that you would hear me forever, but because of the people who are standing here, I say this so that they may believe that you have sent me.' Having said this, he raised his voice and cried out loudly, 'Lazarus, come out here!' (Jn 11:41–43)

Nowhere else, in any of the gospels, do we hear him call out in such a commanding tone.

Called by his name, touched in the I, under his own power, the deceased comes out of the grave. Is this the answer to his question, 'What must I do' (Mk 10:17)? Is the call of Jesus to the people, 'Release him and let him go' (Jn 11:44) speaking in the certainty that Lazarus knows where his path now leads, inseparably at Jesus' side? What Jesus said is fulfilled, 'Then come and accompany me' (Mk 10:21).

The temple leadership will not tolerate among them this man who has risen to a life in Christ, and so they decide to kill Lazarus. Lazarus, whom the Lord loved, was probably one of the first to follow the modern Christian path of encountering the spirit: To have and to ask one's questions; to bear the consequences of the answer in fidelity to oneself; to renounce all that one has lived and secured up to now; to preserve the continuity of one's identity even in the experience of death; to be able to be called upon; to cultivate the courage to go one's own way; to know in which spirit we want to live.

3

Encounters with Christ

Again and again, the question arises of how an encounter with Christ happens today? During his lifetime, this question did not occur to the people of the Holy Land. Or it could have been a different question: Do I want to meet him of whom so many speak?

In the many moving accounts of people whose destiny brought them close to death, we hear of experiences of spiritual encounters.* Such experiences appear in some accounts of Holocaust survivors. These are gifted moments in destiny. But are there verifiable methods that lead to such experiences?

The gospel of the one whom the Lord loved, which we know as the Gospel of John, seems to be written from the depths of such an experience.

Perhaps it is possible to read and explore the paths to be followed towards an encounter with Christ in the human encounters that John describes in more detail. Could a method be found that leads to this goal?

Immediately after the baptism in the Jordan, John reports on the first human encounter with Jesus Christ after that event changed the very basis of his life.

---

* See for instance, Kübler-Ross, *On Life after Death,* or Moody, *Life after Life.*

> The following day John saw Jesus coming towards him and said, 'Take note, he is the Lamb of God who takes upon himself the guilt of this world ... I saw the Spirit of God in the form of a dove descending from the spiritual worlds and remain with him ... I have seen it, and I vouch for it, that this is the Son of God.' (Jn 1:29, 32–34).

John sees the form of a dove and recognises the presence of the Spirit of God. The way he perceives, taking it as truth, leads him to the certainty that the Spirit is near. His vision allows him to become a 'seer'. This is the world of the ancient mysteries of knowledge.

> The following day John stood together again with two of his disciples, and when he looked up, he saw Jesus walking by. Then he said, 'Behold, he is the Lamb of God.' When the two disciples heard his words, they followed Jesus. (Jn 1:35–37)

The two disciples heard their teacher's indication; they understood and acted; they followed. Their realisation leads to action. This is the world of the new mysteries of the will.

> Then Jesus turned to them, looked at them, and said to those who followed him, 'What are you looking for?'
> They said to him, 'Master, where do we find you?'

3. ENCOUNTERS WITH CHRIST

He said, 'Come, and you shall see.' They went with him and realised where he stayed. (Jn 1:38f)

These are the first words that we hear the Son of God speak on earth, and both sentences are worthy of consideration. What – not whom – are you looking for? How well our life would go if we always knew what we were seeking. And how obvious is the misconception that the answer lies in a previously known human relationship.

The second sentence is a true prophecy. Come, break away from the position you have taken and go your way, then you will see anew.

Andrew, one of these first two disciples, 'first found his brother Simon, and he said to him, "We have found the Messiah," that is, the Christ, and he led him to Jesus. Jesus looked at him and said, "You are Simon, the son of John; you shall be called Cephas," that is, the rock.' (Jn 1:41f).

If this, too, is a method of encountering Christ, then we can say: anyone who is securely grounded in themselves and lives in firm trust finds the way to him.

But other ways are also described. 'At the beginning of the next day, Jesus wanted to walk to Galilee, and he met Philip. And Jesus said to him, "Follow me".' (Jn 1:43).

It is not Philip who seeks and finds Christ, but Christ who finds him. Does the gaze of Christ go out over the world to find those who are capable of being called? The healing at the pool of Bethesda tells a similar story.

> It was at the Sheep Gate in Jerusalem, a pool called Bethesda in Hebrew; there were five halls where many people lay powerless, including the blind, the lame, and the emaciated ... A man was there who had already been lying in his weakness for thirty-eight years. Jesus saw him lying there and knew that much time had passed for him. Then Jesus said to him, 'Do you want to receive new powers?' (Jn 5:2–6).

Here, too, Christ sees the single person amid the multitude who are sick.

୶

A curious encounter is also reported immediately after Philip's calling. Philip visits Nathanael, who is sitting under the fig tree and tells him that he has found the Messiah, Jesus, from Nazareth. But Nathanael doubts:

> 'Out of Nazareth? How can salvation come from there?'
> ... Jesus perceived in the spirit the way Nathanael came towards him, and said, 'Behold, he is in truth an Israelite; his spirit is pure.'
> Then Nathanael said to him, 'From where do you know me?'
> Jesus answered and said to him, 'Before

> Philip called you when you were sitting under the fig tree, I perceived you.'
> Nathanael answered him, 'Master, you are truly the Son of God. You are the king of Israel.' (Jn 1:46–49)

The place of the meeting – Nathanael sits under the fig tree – and the words 'a true Israelite', distinguish him insofar as the fig tree was Israel's sacred tree. It was regarded as the paradisal Tree of Knowledge.

The term 'true Israelite' recalls an expression from the initiation rites of the Mithras mysteries. Among the seven degrees of initiation, there was one that required the initiate to expand their consciousness so that they could become the bearer of the folk spirit. This fifth degree of initiation was called 'the Persian', whereby 'Persian' could be synonymous with any folk spirit. It is in this sense that the words 'true Israelite' are to be understood.

In the next encounter, Christ leads a conversation about knowledge with Nicodemus, who comes to him 'in the middle of the night'. They converse about the divine origin of the human being and the power that is to be acquired in life, the power to overcome death so as to be born. Nicodemus is an *archōn*. He belongs to the leading hierarchy of priests, and when he opens the conversation with the words, 'Master, we know that you have come to us as a teacher sent by God' (Jn 3:2), it becomes clear that the temple and its priests were well aware of the importance of Christ Jesus. The discussion, therefore, concentrates straightforwardly on its main theme, being born of the spirit.

'Amen, I tell you the truth. If someone is not born of the life force of water and the breath of the spirit, they cannot enter the Kingdom of God. What is born of the earth remains attached to the earthly nature, but what is born of the spirit is itself spirit.' (Jn 3:5f)

With Nathanael and Nicodemus, both conversations are between knowledgeable people. Their questions can be answered. We also hear this old mystery rule from the mouth of Jesus, 'Anyone who has, it can be given to them, but whoever has not acquired it for themselves, from them shall be taken away even that which they thought they had' (Mk 4:25).

Both Nathanael and Nicodemus do not walk with the disciples but remain with their tasks in Galilee and Jerusalem. Only at Jesus' burial do we meet Nicodemus again (Jn 19:39) and Nathanael only at the last appearance of the Risen Lord at the Sea of Galilee (Jn 21:2).

Following a path of inner training leads to an encounter with God.

In the foreign country of Samaria, at Jacob's well, there is another important encounter. Christ meets a woman who comes to draw water. Both are thirsty, Christ for the water of the earth, the woman for the water of eternal life. Does his thirst quench itself in conversation, speaking and responding from person to person? Does the woman's thirst quench itself in looking at and being able to affirm her destiny and in recognising him, the Lord of Destiny?

3. ENCOUNTERS WITH CHRIST

Turning to Christ with the full confidence that he can bring about a turning point in destiny is also characteristic of the royal official's encounter with Christ at Cana. Concerned for his terminally ill son, he turns to the one he calls *kyrios,* Lord, and asks for help. At first, it seems as if Jesus is stalling him. 'If you do not see visible signs and wonders of the spirit, you do not believe' (Jn 4:48). But the father's renewed, urgent request causes the healing of the boy to happen.

Not only the request for help in one's personal destiny, as was made clear in the case of the Samaritan woman, but also the deep concern for the suffering in other people's destinies, can allow us to seek and walk paths towards an encounter with Christ.

The encounter with Lazarus and his sisters Mary and Martha (Jn 11) was discussed in Chapter 2.

The last, perhaps most extensively described encounter in Christ Jesus' life is that with Pilate, the Roman governor in Israel. Neither side sought this encounter, but there is a strong effort of mutual understanding. It becomes clear that Pilate is trying to save the accused from death, in whom he sees the rightful king of the Jews. To Pilate, Christ Jesus speaks openly about himself in a way that he has never done before with any human being:

> 'My kingdom is not of this world. If I were
> a king on earth, my soldiers would fight to
> prevent me from falling into the hands of the
> Jews. But my kingdom is not of this world.'

> Then Pilate answered him, 'So you are a king?'
> Jesus said, 'You say that I am a king. I was born for this purpose and came into this world to be a witness to the truth. Whoever comes from truth hears my words.
> Then said Pilate to him, 'What is truth?'
> (Jn 18:36–38)

The conversation ends with this question. The dawning consciousness of Europe stepped into Christianity with Pontius Pilate's question about truth. To this day, this question has not lost any of its relevance.

The encounters described occurred in Jesus Christ's lifetime, between his baptism and his death on the cross. Yet not all possibilities for an encounter have been exhausted. Christ's life, as described in John's Gospel, also goes beyond death. The Risen One was close to his followers until his ascension into heaven. And since then? Did his being taken up into heaven mean, at the same time, being taken into our hearts in the sense of his words, 'Behold, God's Kingdom is becoming a reality within you' (Lk 17:21)?

In moving words, Paul speaks of Christ's future new presence in us, his *parousia*. 'He, the God of peace, consecrates your entire being in perfect unity of spirit, soul, and body, that they may be kept in luminous purity on the day of the return of our Lord Jesus Christ' (1Th 5:23).

Are the encounters with the Risen One in John's

3. ENCOUNTERS WITH CHRIST

Gospel precursors of our future interior experience? The forty days between the Resurrection and the Ascension is a special time with the Risen One. Before Easter, it is a question of the Son of God living here on earth in a material human body. After his Ascension, we look up to the Son of God present in God's kingdom and within human beings. For forty days, Christ Jesus, the Son of Man, appears in a subtle body, certainly similar to his appearance on the Mount of Transfiguration. 'Before their eyes, he was transfigured. His face shone like the sun; his garments shone like the light' (Mt 17:2).

The resurrection body of the Son of Man is a transubstantiated earthly body. Its materiality was transformed into a substance that supports life. This is also how Paul describes it: 'A material body will be planted in the earth as seed, but the immortal spiritual body will be awakened' (1Cor 15:44).

First experiences along these paths are shared by those who encounter the Risen One.

The first is Mary Magdalene in her deep pain of being abandoned by her Lord. With tears in her eyes, she turned away from the tomb where she could not find him.

> And she saw Jesus standing there, but did not know it was Jesus. He said to her, 'Woman, what are you wailing about? Whom do you seek?'
> She thought that he was the gardener and said to him, 'Sir, if you have taken him away,

tell me where you have put him, and I will
carry him away.' (Jn 20:14f)

Mary Magdalene turns inwardly from the tomb, which contains only the past and turns towards the one who is speaking to her there. He asks whom she is seeking, what she is wailing about. Facing her and her pain, Christ calls her by name, because in the form he has taken on, she does not recognise him. Being called by name, her eyes open and she recognises her Master. But she must not touch him, because he has not yet risen to his Father (Jn 20:17). Has the pain made her a seer? Has the word that he spoke, he who is the Word, touched her deeply? With what eyes did she see the Risen One? With the eyes of the soul, the eyes of the body? Certainly both.

> Now when it was late on this first day after the Sabbath, and the doors of the disciples' house were shut for fear of the Jews, Jesus came and stood in their midst and said to them, 'Peace be with you.' And speaking thus, he showed them his hands and his side. A joy that they saw the Lord pulsed through the disciples. (Jn 20:19f)

The Lord reappeared to them in a form that none of them recognised – for none of the twelve disciples had yet seen the wounds on his body. In a body that was now able to pass through closed doors, a body not of a coarse material nature, he stepped into their midst and spoke to them of their commission to heal

3. ENCOUNTERS WITH CHRIST

sins. Did the disciples recognise him by his voice, by the pacifying power of his words? 'Joy pulses through them,' says the evangelist because their fearful abandonment had turned into a feeling of happiness and new solidarity.

Is it the common bond with the Lord in the inner space, the closed room, that makes the presence of the living God possible? Is the mystery of Christian community-building, the mystery of his church, addressed here?

In the octave of Easter Sunday, after eight days, the Risen Lord also met Thomas, who had set conditions for his belief. 'If I do not see in his hands the mark of the nails and put my finger in the nail marks and my hand in his side, then I will not take it into myself as truth' (Jn 20:25). And the Risen One grants it, blessing, as it were, the disciple's effort of knowledge through his words: 'Reach out your finger and see my hands. And reach out your hand and put it into my side, and do not disbelieve, but trust in what you feel' (Jn 20:27).

Even reverent efforts of knowledge, which increase to faith, can become a path to an encounter with Christ. 'It is you; you are my Lord and God' (Jn 20:28).

And we are told of a last encounter between the disciples and the Risen One. It culminates in the Risen One's conversation with Peter in the presence of the disciple whom the Lord loved after the early morning meal together at the Sea of Galilee (Jn 21:1–19). All night long, the disciples had tried unsuccessfully to catch fish. With his encouragement, they cast the net again, and it overflows. By this, the disciple 'whom he loved' recognises him. They share bread and fish with the Risen Lord, and then they hear Christ ask Peter three times about his love for him.

These last sentences to his disciples are about two religious capacities that need to be cultivated. Three times he says to Peter, Feed the flock entrusted to you, then you will love me. The other disciple is to 'remain,' to create and preserve a dwelling place in himself, so that the Lord may have a place for his return.

Love of duty and love of faithfulness are also today's paths to Christ. But very different paths lead to an encounter with Christ. There is no single way to God. John's Gospel describes some of them.

4

God's Questions for Human Beings

We question situations or actions that we find inharmonious or in need of change. We find them worthy of questioning. It may be noticed that in the two reports of creation in the Old Testament (Gen 1–2) and the New Testament (Jn 1:1–18), there are no questions; there are only intentional statements.

Among the animals, one was the most alert and practically wise, *phronimōtatos,* the 'most ingenious' as the Greek text calls the serpent. It was the most far-thinking and least satisfied with the actual state of creation and the created human being. The serpent questions the one spiritually mobile part of the human being. 'Is it true that God has said that you shall not eat of every tree of paradise?' (Gen 3:1). Eve does not yet know this form of thinking, and so, undoubtingly and out of deep trust, she repeats word for word what she has heard from God. But she proves no match for the serpent's temptation, who holds out the prospect, 'You will be like God and know what is beautiful and good, and what is reprehensible and evil' (Gen 3:5). The task and the skill of science are to ask questions and set existing knowledge into motion, bringing about future development. It is different from faith, which formulates and expresses for itself what has become a certainty.

A little later, when Adam and Eve try to evade the Creator's eyes out of shame, the Lord takes up this means of knowing and heals the serpent's attack by helping them to a new self-awareness with a question. The first conversation between God and humanity begins with a question. 'Adam, where are you!' (Gen 3:9). And God's question awakens in human beings the knowledge of their actions. The serpent's question creates doubt by illicit means; God's question leads to self-knowledge and awareness.

Such questions from God have a special place in John's Gospel. They characterise Christ's relationship to human beings. (To go into all of Christ's questions in the text would go beyond the scope of this book.) The first and last questions are, as it were, the framework around this web of relationships. In the first chapter, immediately after the account of the baptism in the Jordan, it says that Christ Jesus addresses a question to two of John the Baptist's disciples who follow him. 'What are you looking for?' (Jn 1:38). These are his first words that the text passes on to us. The question 'what' of their search allows the two disciples to become aware of a decisive question: What am I looking for in life?

This is a real question from God, and even today it has not lost its relevance. What am I really looking for? Friends, health, a worthwhile task, the meaning of existence, happiness, money, contentment – what? It is a question worthy of being asked and worth considering.

4. GOD'S QUESTIONS FOR HUMAN BEINGS

At the end of his life, Christ Jesus asks the question differently. Of those who want to take him prisoner, he asks, 'Who are you looking for?' (Jn 18:4). And Mary Magdalene is the first to hear the Risen One speak when he asks her, 'Woman, what are you wailing about? Whom do you seek? (Jn 20:15). The question of the search for *what* leaves the person free to reflect; the question, *Who are you seeking?* puts the one being asked into the earnestness of self-reflection.

At the wedding feast in Cana, we hear Christ again question a person who is very close to him. During the feast, the supply of wine is running out, and Mary the mother, who is among the guests with Jesus and his disciples, turns to her son with the words, 'They have no more wine' (Jn 2:3). The incredibly short answer of Jesus, *ti emoi kai soi, gynai?* (Jn 2:4), is a question. Its translation, 'Woman, what have I to do with thee?' (King James) or 'Woman, why turn to me?' (Catholic Jerusalem Bible) or 'Pay heed, O woman, to the power which flows between me and you' (Madsen), shows once again how difficult it is to translate one language into another; not only to translate with fidelity but also trying to reflect the intention of a text.

The King James Version supplements the completely missing verb in Greek with *have to do*, the Jerusalem Bible with *turn*, Madsen with *the power which flows*. The formulations in the King James and in the Jerusalem translations sound dismissive, almost coarse; the sentence in Madsen's version is interpreted very

39

broadly. Could the key be found in the small word *kai* (and)? Is Christ Jesus concerned to make it clear that he can only help together with his mother since his hour has not yet come? If one emphasises the *with* in the King James translation, the phrase reveals his secret. God does not act on behalf of the human being; Christ Jesus wants to and is only able to work together *with* the human being.

How important the individual's own activity is to Christ becomes clear in the two healings (Jn 5 and Jn 9). The sick man lay in his weakness (Jn 5:5) for thirty-eight years, almost the measure of a life in those days. Christ Jesus saw him lying there and reawakened and strengthened the life force with his question, 'Do you want to regain your strength?' (Jn 5:6).

Not only does the Lord of Destiny's question give a new and decisive direction to what we seek in life, but God's question can also reawaken the lost courage to live. This becomes clear in another way in the healing of the blind man to whom he gives sight and, with it, new certainty of soul. He is the only one who, apart from Christ Jesus himself, can use the great name of God, I AM the I AM, *egō eimi*, for himself (Jn 9:9). Christ's question addresses the power of the self awakening in him:

> 'Do you believe in the Son of Man?'
> He answered and said, 'Who is he, Lord? I want to believe in him.' (Jn 9:35f)

'Do you believe – have faith – in the Son of Man?' says the Greek text, as if faith were a power that can discern what is hidden within.

An important moment in the disciples' life with their Lord is characterised by the question that Christ Jesus addresses to Philip before the feeding of the five thousand. '"Where shall we buy bread that they may eat?" He said this to test him' (Jn 6:5–6). The disciples are to learn to act out of their initiative. Bread represents human work on earth, not merely trusting in heaven's help, such as the manna that fed the people in the desert. The affirmation of our earthly destiny and our love for the earth let us find in life the One who said of himself:

> I am the bread of life. Your fathers ate the manna in the desert and died. This is the bread which comes down from heaven, that everyone may eat of it and not die. I am the bread of life which came down from heaven. Whoever eats of this bread will live in all time. (Jn 6:48–51)

This saying causes a division among those who follow him. Many turn away from him because there is a longing in them that God should act for them and grant them the bread from heaven (Jn 6:31) rather than that they should follow the path of faith that Christ shows them: 'This is the work of the spirit, that you turn in faith to him whom God has sent' (Jn 6:29).

In rising uncertainty, even the twelve have to face his question, 'And you, do you also want to go away?' But in them, the power of faith in him has already become the knowledge of his divinity so that Peter can answer for all, 'Lord, to whom shall we go? The power of your words awakens eternal life. And we have believed and recognised that you are the Holy One of God' (Jn 6:67–69).

This new faith, which is not a simple perception of truth, but is acquired through the attentive perception of the senses and tested in cognition, could be adopted by the people who met Christ Jesus because in him they encountered in earthly reality the identity of spirit and substance, of God's being and human being.

But this faith must be acquired and cultivated. It is not simply a gift. Christ asks several times how this power is being cultivated. Thus he asks Martha, Lazarus' sister, 'Anyone who finds trust in me will find life in death, and every living person who believes in me will not suffer death through all time. Do you believe that?' In her, too, the power of faith has already increased to knowledge, and she answers, 'Yes Lord, I believe, and I have come to know that you are Christ, the Son of God, who came into the world' (Jn 11:25–27).

The conversation of Jesus Christ with his disciple Philip on the evening of Holy Thursday shows how difficult it is to make the power of faith last.

> Philip asks, 'Lord, make the Father visible to us; that will be enough for our soul.'
> And Jesus said to him, 'So long have I been

> with you now, and you have not recognised me, Philip? Whoever sees me sees the Father. How can you say, "Let us see the Father?" Is your trust not founded on the fact, I in the Father – the Father in me?' (Jn 14:8–10)

And later in the evening, he speaks to all the disciples.

> You think that you now have faith? Consider this, first of all, the hour is coming, and it has already come, when you must be separated from one another and scattered, each one to his own being. (Jn 16:31f)

Faith acquired through knowledge is an act of man's spirit-given self. This faith cannot be transferred to another. We can believe in another person, never for another person.

In the Risen One's last meeting with his disciples at the Sea of Galilee, the Lord asks the last questions, and he asks them three times, 'Simon, son of John, do you love me?' (Jn 21:15–17). And Peter affirms it three times.

From Christ Jesus' first question about what we are looking for in life to his last question about our love for him, his questions range widely: search – recognise – believe – love. These are four capacities to be acquired by our God-seeking soul.

5

The Secret of the Centre

It is not difficult to see how contested the middle, the centre, is everywhere. Be it the middle between one human being and another, the so fragile human relationship; be it one's own centre, which is not easy to find and protect from attacks; be it the ever-mentioned, often painfully experienced upheavals that can occur in mid-life. We all know how difficult it is for us to be able to convey a mediating, well-balanced judgment.

In Christianity, the centre is particularly emphasised, because at the centre of our faith is the cross, the life-death sign of Jesus Christ. The centre point of a church is the altar, the place where what happened on Golgotha at Easter is continued. And in the middle of the altar, stand the chalice and paten, bread and wine.

In the Gospel of John, the centre is a fundamental motif that characterises the work of Christ and the Christians.

It is John the Baptist who first lets this motif resound. 'He who comes after me is already working in your midst, and you do not recognise him' (Jn 1:26) because this 'midst' is occupied. The Law of Moses and his guidance of the people took up the inner space of human experience, for God directed the fate of his people from afar. Anyone who wished

5. THE SECRET OF THE CENTRE

to see God close up would have wished for death, for God had said, 'You cannot see my face, for no one who sees me lives' (Ex 33:20). And now John the Baptist speaks of the fact that 'he is already working in your midst'. The distant God has come close. God takes the initiative towards us human beings, and not just the other way round, from us towards him. With our senses, we can perceive his closeness and then also recognise him, for nothing can become the content of our recognition that has not previously been the activity and content of our perception. Our consciousness is the mirror where our perception and our thinking meet, and the cleaner this mirror is, the clearer the contents of our mind are. Our daily effort is to keep the mirror of our consciousness clean.

At the autumn Feast of Tabernacles, at Michaelmas, John's Gospel reports a second time about an event of the middle. Among the religious feasts of the year, the Feast of Tabernacles is a joyful feast. For seven days, the people celebrate the coming beginning of the cool, rainy winter season with sacrifices of thanksgiving and songs of praise. 'But the Jews sought him in the feast days and said, Where might he be?' Will he come to share our lives? May he share in our joy, our hope, our praise of God? And then he is present when the festival reaches its midpoint, teaching the people, so that they wonder in amazement, 'How does he know the Scriptures, never having studied?' (Jn 7:15). His teaching reaches its climax on the last day, which gives the feast with its solemn processions a special splendour. Not only will God soon give the clouds of heaven rain for the thirsty earth again, but he, Christ Jesus, will become a life-giving spring.

> 'Anyone who thirsts, come to me and drink. To those who believe in me, it shall be done according to the Scriptures: "Rivers of living water will flow from their bodies".' This he said about the Holy Spirit, whom all who believe in him should receive (Jn 7:37f)

The trust that is based on the concrete perception of the deeds and words of Jesus Christ, a knowing faith in the reality of the spirit, makes a human being a source of life. Our Christianity does not belong to us alone; it belongs to the world in which we live and for which we live.

In the eighth chapter of John's Gospel, the motif of the centre especially comes to the fore. It tells of Christ Jesus' encounter with a woman in the temple. 'The scribes and the Pharisees led a woman before him who had been caught in a breach of marriage. They placed her in the middle' (Jn 8:3) and brought charges against her.

The guilty human being is in the middle, not Christ Jesus; it is a true image of the cause of his incarnation. And the guardians of the Law say to him. 'Teacher ... in our Law, Moses commanded that such be stoned. We want to hear what you say.' (Jn 8:4f). And they hear that he confirms the Law but expands it so that everyone must examine themselves

5. THE SECRET OF THE CENTRE

and their own actions. '"Let him who is without sin be the first to throw a stone at her" ... And they went out, one by one; the elders went first, and Jesus was left alone with the woman in the middle.' (Jn 8:7–9). The Son of God is alone; in the middle stands the sinful human being, held and encouraged by his presence. 'I do not condemn you. Go your way; from now on, sin no more.' (Jn 8:11). His trust strengthens us along our paths. His word is an encouragement when our courage fails.

Only after completing his earthly life on the cross on Golgotha do we again hear about the middle. 'There they crucified him and with him two others, one on the right, the other on the left, but Jesus in the middle' (Jn 19:18).

But it was not only then in Jerusalem at the Place of the Skull that Christ Jesus was in the midst of those who accompanied him; since then, he has been at the centre of the earth's development. The cross, whose dark shadow fell on a blooming spring world, has become the primordial sign of our human and Christian existence. We place ourselves in existence, upright between earth and heaven, indissolubly belonging to the earth and, at the same time, connected to the world above us, with wide-open arms turning towards and receiving the whole of creation. In his *Hymns to the Night,* Novalis calls the cross a victory banner of our human breed. In the sacrament, the mystery of transubstantiation takes place under the sign of three crosses over bread and wine. We also inscribe the holy sign of the cross on our midline confessing the triune God and his blessing. Jesus Christ – the centre: this is the basic statement of Christianity.

In the account of the first meeting of the Risen Lord with the disciples on the evening of Easter, it becomes clear how important this motif of the centre is to the evangelist.

> When it was late on this first day after the Sabbath, and the doors to the disciples were shut for fear of the Jews, Jesus came and stood in their midst and said to them, 'Peace be with you.' (Jn 20:19)

Without question, John is describing the room of the house in which the disciples gathered that evening. It could have been the room of the Last Supper on Mount Zion in Jerusalem, where the disciples locked themselves in out of fear. And yet the Lord enters through the closed door into their midst. Does he thereby, at the same time, also enter a completely different space in their midst, an inner space of consciousness that is firmly closed and filled with fear, and which he calms with his words and fills with joy?

At the beginning of the Gospel (1:26), John the Baptist said, 'He is already working in your midst, and you do not recognise him.' Now he steps into their midst, and the disciples recognise him. What happened to the centre of the human being? Can it become a heart organ for a new sense?

One of the disciples is missing that evening, Thomas, who reacts with skepticism to the disciples' news:

5. THE SECRET OF THE CENTRE

The other disciples told him, 'We have seen the Lord.'

But he replied, 'If I do not see the imprint of the nails in his hands and put my finger on the place of the nails and my hand in his side, I will not take it up as the truth.' (Jn 20:25).

And in the octave of the Easter evening, when the disciples are together again in the inner room, the Lord steps once more into their midst and through his words blesses Thomas' efforts to gain knowledge and since then, certainly, also every seeking person's striving for knowledge.

Seven times Christ Jesus shows himself as the one present in the middle, fulfilling his word, 'Where two or three are united in my name, then I am in their midst' (Mt 18:20). He, the Word, is the connecting centre from person to person.

6

The Tidings of Becoming

The tidings of becoming sound forth to us from the first beginnings of the creation of the world. 'God said, "Let there be ..." and there was ... And God looked on all that he had made, and behold, it was very good' (Gn 1:3, 31); for in all things that are, God is powerfully present, he, the One and Only, the Almighty.

But the only creatures given the gift of development are human beings. 'Let us create the human being, an image that is like us' (Gen 1:26); that is, not already created equal, but only becoming equal in the course of his development. And through human work, the whole of creation was to have a share in this development, for the human's task was to cultivate and protect the completed garden (Gn 2:15).

To be self-creating and to transform creation is therefore connected with our humanity. None of us are finished as we are. Are we already truly Christian, or are we making an effort to become so?

Inherent in all becoming, in all development, is the necessity of passing away. How could something new be created if the existing did not perish?

The Gospel of John often speaks of becoming in the sense of coming into being and developing. The all-inclusive spiritual content of the world *ho logos* and the creative will of God unite, and *panta*, everything,

6. THE TIDINGS OF BECOMING

is created, which now develops and reveals itself further as life and light. It develops further as the human being with the goal of becoming God-like, as a created world. The whole variety of what came into being is crowned with the sentence, 'And the Word became flesh and dwelt among us' (Jn 1:14), and through Christ Jesus, the Logos has become the creator of grace and truth.

The first spiritual sign, which Christ Jesus performs at the wedding in Cana, also speaks of development through transformation. When the guests lack wine, he orders the servants to fill the water jugs with fresh water, then to draw from the water and to bring it to the master of the feast.

> When the master of the feast tasted the water that had been turned into wine, he called the bridegroom, for he did not know where the wine came from, since only the servants who drew the water knew. (Jn 2:9)

The servants drew water and also know that it is water, but the master of the feast tastes wine when he drinks the water *that has become wine*. When did it become this? External contact with Christ Jesus, which could have brought about this transformation, had not happened. Does it happen within the master of the feast who drinks water and feels the effect of the wine in himself? Does transformation take place simultaneously, from the inside outward, from the spiritual to the substances of the earth?

૪

This process is described even more clearly in the encounter of Christ with the Samaritan woman at the well. The well where the two of them meet only provides the water that quenches the thirst of everyday life. But an encounter with Christ may open up closed sources of eternal human life.

> Everyone who drinks the water from this well will thirst again. But whoever drinks of the water that I give him, their thirst will be quenched for all time, for the water that I give to someone will become in them a spring, from which the continuous life will spring forth. (Jn 4:13f)

When a person begins to act from their I and to direct their destiny, then they will become a life-giving source for the world in which they live. But if they are unable to hold onto their innermost self, then fear will take hold of them.

This is how John describes it in Chapter 6. In the experience of the feeding of the five thousand, the day was very moving for the disciples, because, as the evangelist Mark points out, the Lord had said to his disciples, 'You yourselves give to people the food they need' (Mk 6:37), but they could not. Did this incapacity accompany the disciples on their way into the night? 'Deep darkness ruled, and Jesus had not yet come to them' (Jn 6:17). And then, when the

6. THE TIDINGS OF BECOMING

elements began to rage, 'They were afraid, and they beheld how Jesus walked over the sea until he came close to their boat' (Jn 6:19). He came close, *engys ginomenon* the Greek says. Its strong, miraculous power speaks. If the day's events have not yet been processed and 'make waves' when it is night, then with the power of his I, Christ steps of his own accord alongside the inexperienced and calms the storm. '"I AM, fear not." And when they wanted to take him into the boat, the boat was on land, exactly where they wanted to go.' (Jn 6:20f). We urgently need the power of trust in Christ to be able to get where we want to go.

To receive Christ into our boat with full trust is one thing; it is another not to lose sight of the goal of our development, which he describes to us with the words, 'Trust in the light as long as it shines upon you, that you may become sons of light' (Jn 12:36). And this also means becoming *his* sons, because he is the light of the world.

Christ speaks these words to some Greeks who have come to Jerusalem for the Passover, to see him with their own eyes and then to be able to recognise and believe that he is the Messiah. A faith that grows as the fruit of knowledge is the faith that truly surrenders to the living God and knows that it is united with him. Christ speaks of this fruit of a knowing faith in the Farewell Discourse.

> If you keep me in you and the powers of thought that emanate from me remain with you, then you will be able to ask whatever you want, and it will be given to you. In this, my

Father is first revealed in that you yield rich fruit of the spirit, and thus become my true disciples. (Jn 15:7f)

By granting Christ space to exist within themselves, natural human beings are born as new humans through working on themselves in their thoughts and then also in their actions, *and thus become my true disciples,* who know themselves to be faithfully connected to the future development of Christianity in the world.

The tidings of development are an announcement about the triune God, 'who is, who was and who is to come' (Rv 1:4); for God is not only one who is for all eternity. Becoming and transforming are also inherent in him. He is the living present, the one who exists from eternity and the one who reveals himself anew in all the future of the earth.

The tidings of becoming are at the same time a message about the human being, who is, who was, and who will become.

7
Not Yet

Our relationship to time is multifaceted. When we speak of our lifetime, we mean something quite different from when we speak of time according to the clock. A lifetime is the time period that is ours to shape. Clock time, on the other hand, is measurable time, which is always measured precisely in ever smaller units. Our inner mood towards time is also fundamentally different. With a certain inner tension, we await the periods of 'not yet' that are still closed to us and look with satisfaction or resignation at the time that has now passed and can no longer be influenced.

We experience our actions and thoughts as divided into past, present and future, and try hard to grasp the present moment consciously.

In the same way, John, the writer of the Book of Revelation, characterises the nature of what he wants to bring to the churches: 'Grace be with you and peace from him who is, who was and who is to come' (Rv 1:4). He is the One present; he has been since the beginning of time, and he will be so in all future times on earth – the omnipresent One.

The One who appears confirms this description of his being and expands it with the words, 'I am the Alpha and the Omega, the original beginning and the end of the world' (Rv 1:8). All being and all development are united in him.

With the baptism in the Jordan River, this divine being entered into the time stream of the earth. He submitted to the laws of measurable time, to becoming and passing away, to the destiny of the earth. This is how Paul describes it in his Letter to the Philippians (2:6–8):

> He was divine in form, but he did not claim his divinity. He emptied himself and took on the form of one who served. He became a man among men, recognised as a man through his appearance. Thus he bowed under earthly being, willing to follow it unto death, death on the cross.

Three quite different principles of order for time are found in John's Gospel. The expression most frequently used there is *hōra*, that is, the time granted to the I, the ego, who can fill it with life and activity. This is how the ancient Greeks understood *hōra* to mean not only the appropriate time for action but also a very specific hour of the day, as well as the hour of youth that has developed into its most beautiful blossoming; the hour of the ripening of fully developed humanity; the awakening of nature in its highest harmonious beauty.

We use this word in a similar sense when, for example, we ask a person for one hour of their time, and do not mean a span of sixty minutes. Or when we hear Christ Jesus ask on the night of betrayal, 'Did you not have the strength to watch with me for an hour?' (Mt 26:40).

The other word for time, *kairos*, refers to the

right moment to be seized, the now of the event, the presence of the spirit: 'When the time was right, the angel of the Lord came down into the pool' (Jn 5:4).

If the natural conditions of the spring pond made it possible, when the right time came, the spirit being could connect with the water to make it bubble up and thus turn it into a healing spring. Spiritual beings cannot become effective in the earthly world simply at any arbitrary time. The *kairos* must be prepared.

The third word for time the Greeks commonly used was *chronos,* measurable time, the determinable course of time through which an earlier and later, a 'not yet' and an 'already now', is created.

This 'not yet' also has its meaning in Christ Jesus' life. Do not the first thirty years of Jesus of Nazareth stand under the sign of the not yet incarnated Son of God? For only at the baptism in the Jordan does the voice from the heavens sound, 'You are my Son, the beloved; in you, I will reveal myself' (Mk 1:11).

But also in his life's further course, Christ Jesus speaks of a 'not yet' of his effectiveness, for example, at the wedding at Cana (Jn 2:4). When the guests lack wine and his mother tells him this, he says to her, 'What shall be done by me and what by you, O woman? My hour has not yet come.' The time when he can work only from within himself without the mediation of a human being has not yet been fulfilled. His answer is not a rejection of his mother, meaning 'what business is it of yours?' but rather the question indicates the mystery of a future transformation, the

'Christ-ening' of the Earth, which Christ, with the participation of humanity, has come to fulfill. The first human being on earth, who is existentially and completely involved in this work of redemption, is Jesus of Nazareth. In the conversation with his mother at the wedding in Cana, however, the 'and' in Christ Jesus' question – *ti emoi kai soi,* 'what through me and through you' – also addresses and confirms this working together through the following 'not yet': 'My hour has not yet come.'

The fact that such a 'not yet' can exist at all in Christ Jesus' life and activity is remarkable and makes it clear that the incarnation of the Son of God is not a single occurrence, but a development that began with the baptism in the Jordan and was completed with the Crucified One saying, 'It is finished' (Jn 19:30).

The hour in which the 'not yet' is fulfilled and Christ Jesus has to act completely on his own, is the hour of his death, in which also the certainty that 'I and the Father are one' (Jn 10:30) will begin to answer the question, 'My God, My God, why have you forsaken me?' (Mt 27:46).

On Monday of Holy Week, when the Greeks in Jerusalem asked Philip, 'Sir, we want to see Jesus' (Jn 12:21), Christ Jesus replied and spoke to them with a parable of his death.

> The hour has come that the Son of Man will be revealed in his true form. Amen, the truth I tell you. Only when the grain of wheat is

7. NOT YET

laid in the ground and dies does it bear much fruit; if it does not die, it remains unchanged.' (Jn 12:23f)

He himself had also been moved by this now-revealed secret of his life and mission: 'Now my soul is shaken. What can I say? Father, save me from this hour?' (Jn 12:27). It is an hour of deepest paradox in Christ Jesus' life, in which he asks himself whether he should ask the Father for redemption from death on earth. But he has the strength to be aware that his whole earthly path has led him to this hour, and that he has walked this path step by step: 'But this is why I have approached this hour.' This strength allows him to make another request. 'Father, reveal your name' (Jn 12:28). In other words, 'Let your holy name, I AM the I AM, shine forth in me and in every person who wants to unite with me.'

In the final gathering with his disciples on Holy Thursday, Christ's hour finds its radiant fulfilment in the words of the High Priestly Prayer. 'Father, the hour has come; let your Son's essence be made manifest so that in the Son's working, your fatherly being may be revealed' (Jn 17:1). In the Son's suffering of death and victory over death, God the Father, the foundation of all existence, will also be revealed anew. Through Christ Jesus' sacrificial death, the transformation of the earthly-material body, created by God, into a new living bodily form, the resurrection body, will be able to take place. That this mystery will also fulfil itself over time has been clear since Jesus Christ's first proclamation of the Passion to the disciples:

> The Son of Man must suffer much. By the elders, the chief priests and scribes, he will be ostracised and killed, but after three days, he will rise again. (Mk 8:31)

Regarding the resurrection, only in the Gospel of Mark do we find the wording, *after three days*. The Gospels of Matthew and Luke speak of the third day. Such a specific reference to time is missing in the Gospel of John.

How shall we count the three days of the completion of Jesus Christ's earthly life through his death and resurrection? When do the three holy days of the Mystery of Golgotha begin and when are they completed? This question arises through the 'not yet' in the Risen One's conversation with Mary Magdalene on Easter morning, with his words, 'Do not touch me, for I am not yet risen to my Father. Go to my brothers and tell them, I am ascending to my Father' (Jn 20:17).

This period of three days was already known before Christian times from the mysteries, the initiation places, and their rites. Eleusis celebrated its annual dedication on three consecutive days in the middle of the month of Boedromion (September).* From the Old Testament, we know the fate of the prophet Jonah, who dwelt within the great fish to atone for his disobedience to God's command. 'And

---

* See Kerényi, *Die Mysterien von Eleusis*, p. 73.

7. NOT YET

Jonah was in the body of the fish for three days and three nights' (Jon 1:17). Christ Jesus points to this event for the crowd that demands a sign from him:

> The human race of today is a wicked one. They seek a spiritual sign, and no other proof of the spirit can be given to them but the sign of Jonah. Just as Jonah became a spiritual sign for the inhabitants of Nineveh, so will the Son of Man be for the people of today. (Lk 11:29f)

The three days that Jonah needed for clarifying his destiny will also be of decisive importance in the life of Jesus Christ. And did not the Lord also wait three full days until he called the beloved friend, Lazarus, from death into life on the fourth day?

If we take a closer look at the three days, Friday, Saturday and Sunday in their chronological sequence, it becomes clear that Good Friday, the day of Jesus Christ's death, begins with the sunset on the evening of Holy Thursday. It is the time of farewell and the institution of the sacrament at the Last Supper through Jesus Christ's words, 'Take it, this is my body ... this is my blood' (Mk 14:22, 24), 'Do this when you unite yourselves with me in your inward being' (Lk 22:19). Beginning the three days with the Last Supper is at the same time the transubstantiation of his body and blood into substances of this earth, into bread and wine. This transubstantiation begins in the spiritual realm through Jesus Christ's word.

If we count one day further from this hour, we come to Friday evening. On Golgotha, the burial has been completed. The earthly body of Jesus Christ had been lowered into the tomb, surrendered to the forces of earthly decay. The first creation has passed. The Sabbath, the day of rest in the tomb, has begun. On this second day, Christ Jesus enters the kingdom of the dead and becomes the redeemer of the souls of the dead. With sunset on Holy Saturday, the third day begins, the day of resurrection, on which, at dawn, Mary Magdalene finds Jesus Christ's tomb open and is the first to encounter the Risen One.

In this early morning hour, as the Risen One's 'not yet' to Mary Magdalene makes clear, the three days have not yet passed, and the resurrection has not yet been completed. The Risen One's descent into the kingdom of the prince of this world and overcoming of death have been accomplished, but his ascent to the Father is still to come. 'I have not yet ascended to my Father' (Jn 20:17).

Only on the evening of the same day, Easter Sunday, does the Lord reveal himself to the circle of disciples in his new body as the One who rose from death. The disciples recognise him through the wounds on his hands and on his side. Mary Magdalene had still seen the Lord in the morning in the form of a gardener. In the evening after the completion of the three days, the disciples recognise him in his new bodily form through the wounds on his hands and side. Ascending to the Father forms this body through a new unity of the threefold divinity of the Father, the Son, and the Holy Spirit. This form is no longer subject to the earthly material laws.

> When it was late on this first day after the Sabbath, and the doors to the disciples were

7. NOT YET

shut for fear of the Jews, Jesus came and stood in their midst.(Jn 20:19)

The three days began with the institution of the sacrament, the transubstantiation of bread and wine into the body and blood of Christ; they are completed with the creation of Jesus Christ's resurrection body.

The new creation is completed and can be newly accomplished and increased in every sacramental transubstantiation by us Christians.

The 'not yet' in Jesus Christ's earthly life has become his continuing work in the sacraments of his church.

8

The Working of Grace

Old English penny coins were valid currency. They had passed through countless hands, used as the equivalent for countless goods. They never lost their known value, which everyone acknowledged, even when the year of their minting and the queen or king's portrait had long since become unrecognisable. Eventually they were taken out of circulation and replaced by smaller, handier coins.

Such much-used and partly worn out means of payment also exist in religious life. They are our time-honoured concepts of guilt and redemption, grace and mercy, blessing and damnation. They are certainly necessary for our language, and yet they are constantly seeking to be known and used in a new way.

We often use the word grace in the sense of showing mercy before justice: we are all sinners, but God will be merciful.

In the Prologue to his gospel, John speaks about grace quite differently. Not only do we receive grace upon grace out of God's omnipotence, his *plērōma*, but 'grace and truth came into being through Jesus Christ' (Jn 1:17).

Human beings first perceived in Jesus Christ the unhidden unity of spirit and substance, the unveiled appearance of the spiritual essence in an earthly

8. THE WORKING OF GRACE

human being. At the time of Christ, this was a new experience of the truth, in Greek *alētheia,* meaning *unhidden,* for God appeared before the senses in a human being.

In the working of grace, are both the human and the divine, not only God alone, involved? Are not the life and actions of Jesus Christ a picture of this working together? Ever since a human being walked this path in him for the first time, he has been a guide on the path of grace.

Among all creatures, human beings are the only ones who can work in freedom and develop themselves. For this, animals need their instinct or the help of humans. No lion can decide to become a vegetarian, not even with effort. It would be its death. Human beings can change habits out of insight, because nature or their genetic structure does not determine them alone: they also have their own will.

In this sense, we hear Christ Jesus say, 'Behold, you have been healed, sin no more, lest greater evil befall you' (Jn 5:14). That humanity can do this is the first grace.

The first healing that John the evangelist reports describes a further stage in a dynamic concept of grace. To a person who has suffered from his illness for decades and must experience again and again how others get well, Christ says, '"Arise, take up your pallet and go your way." And immediately, the man was healed, took up his pallet, and walked' (Jn 5:8f).

Is it not a mercy for our destiny that we can bear the consequences of our actions and that there can be no institution that relieves us of the consequences of our actions? This is the basis of all penal legislation, which aims at allowing people to come to an understanding of their deeds and to redefine their life's direction. The question is, when does the carrying of the consequences end? After a fixed time? After a change of heart and mind has taken place? With death? In his Second Letter to the Corinthians (5:10), Paul points to an even greater dimension:

> All our nature will be revealed when we
> ascend to the place where Christ works.
> Everyone will then be able to receive and bear
> the just consequences of their earthly deeds,
> whether they are good or evil.

That Christ's will takes the consequences of our earthly life into a future development is the second grace.

Chapter 6 of John's Gospel impressively describes how human actions and God's actions complement each other.

> A great crowd of people followed the Master
> with his disciples because they saw the signs
> of the spirit that he performed on the sick ...
> He asked Philip, 'Where shall we buy bread so
> that they may eat?' (Jn 6:2, 5)

8. THE WORKING OF GRACE

Does bread here stand for what humans can acquire only by working the earth? In temperate latitudes, a year's work must be done, from sowing grain to baking bread, before we can eat a piece of bread. The people have five barley loaves and two fish, and the disciple Andrew asks the Lord, 'What does this mean for so many?' (Jn 6:9).

> Then Jesus took the loaves, blessed them and gave them to the disciples, and the disciples gave them to those who were seated. (Jn 6:11)

Without sharing the disciples' concern that the bread would not be enough, Jesus took what the people had worked for, gave thanks, and gave the bread to the disciples to distribute to the people. 'And they ate and were all satisfied' (Mk 6:42).

Here, the Greek uses the word *eucharistein* for the prayer of thanksgiving. Christ blesses the bread and adds something of his grace, his fullness of existence, to what people give him. He completes the sacrifice of the people with his blessing and transforms it for them into a life-affirming closeness and union with him.

This is the third grace: that God accepts without judgment what we have worked for in life and adds his essence to our deeds as provisions for a future life.

On Holy Thursday at the Last Supper, Christ speaks of the fact that in the future, the disciples will continue his works in faithful solidarity with him.

> Yes, I tell you, amen, those who in trust unite themselves with me will also do the works that I do, and greater works will they do because I go to the Father. (Jn 14:12)

We can be overawed to hear that our works will be greater than the works of the Son of God. Is an explanation to be found in the words, 'for I go to the Father'? What Christ Jesus accomplished in life happened in constant unity of being with the Father who sent him. The things that we human beings do, we must do out of God's will in union with Christ, and this is greater than acting in uninterrupted unity with God.

This is the next stage of God's work of grace. The human being is chosen as God's co-worker in the world and for the world, 'because creation waits in longing for the revelation of the sons of God within humanity' (Rom 8:19).

But not only are God's works for creation's redemption to be continued by humanity, but also the spiritual goals, the thoughts of God, are entrusted by Christ to the human capacity for knowledge. 'All that I have heard from the Father, I have presented for your recognition' (Jn 15:15). Everything. Beyond that there is nothing; that is the *plērōma*, the fullness of the Godhead. This has been accessible to human recognition since the God-consciousness of Christ lived in the human consciousness of Jesus of Nazareth. Human cognition and consciousness have become God's field of action on earth. The *revelation* of God, in Greek *doxa*, and human *thinking cognition*, in Greek *dokein*, are of the same nature.

8. THE WORKING OF GRACE

The two disciples John and Thomas show how differently individuals can handle this ability.

On Easter morning, John hurries to the tomb, finds the tomb empty, 'and what he saw became his inner certainty in faith' (Jn 20:8). On the Sunday after Easter, Thomas met the Risen Lord among the disciples, to whom he had said, 'Unless I have tangible proof by touching the Risen Lord, I will not believe.' And the Lord grants it and thus leads Thomas to the recognition and affirmation, 'It is you, my Lord and my God' (Jn 20:28).

Finally, in the High Priestly Prayer, the goal of this development becomes clear in the words of Jesus Christ: 'Father, I want those you have given me to be with me where I am' (Jn 17:24).

The human being will be taken up into the divine sphere of power and will 'sit on my throne' (Rv 3:21), and 'I will become his God, and he shall be a son to me' (Rv 21:7). Humanity will be raised to a new hierarchy, the hierarchy of the Sons of Man. 'God will work in their midst, and those who are devoted to God will be with him' (Rv 21:3).

The highest perfection of the working of grace is Christ's permeation of creation, into humanity and through humanity into the substances of the earth through transubstantiation in the sacrament.

9

Becoming the Son of Man

We associate the words Son of Man with the name Christ Jesus called himself during his life. The people who met him called him Son of God, son of Joseph, Messiah, Master. Although he spoke of his Father in the heavens who sent him, he spoke of himself as the Son of Man.

At the same time, this word designates the human being's goal: to become a Son of Man. This appears in the Revelation to John in these words, 'Anyone who overcomes themselves will have a share [in eternal life]; I will be their God, and they shall be a son to me' (Rv 21:7).

Through his double sacrifice, Jesus of Nazareth is the first one to reach this goal. In the baptism in the Jordan, the Son of God, Christ, sacrifices his divinity and enters into incarnation on earth as a human being. This is how the Prologue of John's Gospel describes it: 'And the Word became flesh and dwelt among us' (Jn 1:14). And Paul, in the Letter to the Philippians (2:6f):

> He was divine in form, but he did not claim his divinity. He emptied himself and took the form of the servant. He became a man among men, recognised as a man by his bearing.

At the same time, the earthly man Jesus sacrificed his natural humanity to become gradually permeated by Christ in the sense of the word from the Prologue: Christ 'became flesh'. This sacrifice was completed with the words of the Crucified One, 'It is finished' (Jn 19:30).

Because, for the first time, a human being became the Son of Man in Jesus of Nazareth, all of us who strive for discipleship, that is, who want to lead our lives as Christians, can follow this path recorded by John in his gospel.

The appearance of the Son of Man was familiar to the pious people of Israel. It had been revealed to the prophet Daniel in powerful images: 'I saw a face in the night and behold there came one in the clouds of heaven like the Son of Man' (Dan 7:13).

So an enlightened human being, graced by God, was the first to receive the tidings.

Furthermore, in the Gospel of John, Christ Jesus does not speak to the people about the Son of Man from the beginning. Instead, he reveals this mystery to two specially prepared people. In Chapter 3, we have spoken of Nathanael and Nicodemus. Nathanael is invited to 'Come and see' (Jn 1:46) the divine being, the Messiah, in his earthly, sense-perceptible realisation. It is not only in the heights of heaven that God reveals himself but also as a human being among humans, as Jesus of Nazareth. And Christ Jesus teaches him: 'The spirit worlds will open before your eyes, and you will see the angels of God ascending and descending on the Son of Man' (Jn 1:51).

The first thing we hear about the Son of Man is that he is an earthly incarnated spiritual being with whom the angels of God, the hierarchies, are in communication. What do they bring down to him out of spiritual heights? What do they carry with them into heaven?

In the nocturnal conversation with Nicodemus, the issue is the question of rebirth in life. He asks Christ, 'How should a man be born anew when he is old? Surely he cannot be conceived a second time in his mother's womb and be born anew?' (Jn 3:4).

To be conceived within and be born anew – is this not a delicate resonance of the Mary mystery of humanity? The virginal human soul gives birth to the spirit child within.

But in the conversation with Nicodemus, Christ Jesus does not only speak about the birth of the Son of Man, whose true home is heaven; he also points to his death. This death of the Son of Man happens according to earthly laws but is also an exaltation, 'As Moses once raised the image of the serpent in the desert as a sign, so the Son of Man must also be raised' (Jn 3:14).

In the Son of Man, creation, fallen to the death of matter, is raised to a new connection with God and redeemed.

The second message we receive about the Son of Man is that a power is born in human beings that can raise their earthly humanity to God, to consecrate it.

To those prepared, this much could be revealed about the Son of Man.

༄

9. BECOMING THE SON OF MAN

John further reports about two people who are enabled by their destiny to learn about the development of the Son of Man through Christ Jesus. One of them, weakened by his illness, had waited many years to be helped by other people to reach the source of healing. Here Christ's question comes to him: 'Do you want to regain your strength?' (Jn 5:6). If you are willing to become one who learns to develop and thereby recover, then 'Stand up, take up your pallet, and set out on your path' (Jn 5:8).

Addressed in his I and awakened in his will, 'the man was healed, took his pallet, and walked' (Jn 5:9).

Christ Jesus, as the Son of Man, brings about decisions for the future by awakening and strengthening courage for destiny.

> Just as life is secure in the Father, so it flows in the Son, because the Father gave it to him. And he gave him the authority as the Son of Man to bring about the decision. (Jn 5:26f)

The second person described was blind from birth and thus lived in a special relationship with the world and other human beings. The healing that Christ Jesus performs on him positions him in his existence in a new, changed way. The answer to the question about the cause of this blindness, 'Who sinned, that he was born blind?' (Jn 9:2), is unimportant. What is important is an unhindered vision and knowledge of the power of God's grace through Christ Jesus that 'is to be made visible in his [the blind man's] being' (Jn 9:3). Is the power of God's grace revealed in the manner and method of healing?

> With these words, he spat on the ground, mixed his saliva with the dust of the earth, spread the clay on the blind man's eyes and said, 'Go now and wash yourself' ... He went and washed himself and came back seeing
> (Jn 9:6f)

Or is it a new self-awareness that is awakened in the healed person, which makes the power of God's grace openly visible in him? He uses a formulation about himself that otherwise only Christ Jesus uses for himself *(egō eimi,* Jn 9:9), that is, I AM the I AM. This newly experienced power of the self then also carries him through what happens to him with the Pharisees. 'They expelled him [from their community]' (Jn 9:34).

In this state of all-on-his-own, Christ Jesus meets him again and asks him:

> 'Do you believe in the Son of Man?'
> He answered and said, 'Who is he, Sir? I want to believe in him.'
> Then Jesus said to him, 'Your eyes have seen him, and he who now speaks to you is he.'
> (Jn 9:35–37).

Is this self-discovery of his eternal being, and his faith in the Son of Man, the revelation of the divine power that is to appear in humanity?

Christ awakens in human beings the organ to recognise the Son of Man and the power to want to connect our destiny with him. This is the third message about the Son of Man.

9. BECOMING THE SON OF MAN

೯

Up to now, Christ Jesus spoke about the Son of Man to learned individuals, prepared by their destiny. Before he began to talk about this mystery to the disciples and the crowds, he entered a new kind of connection with humanity through the feeding of the five thousand. The bread that people had acquired as the fruit of their work on the earth, he had taken into his hands, blessed and thereby filled it with his healing word; he transformed it and gave it to people as food for the journey.

The next morning the people sought him and found him among his disciples on the shore of the Sea of Galilee. These people had walked to him on the mountain near Tiberias. They had experienced the miracle of the feeding and replenishment through him. They had travelled by night to meet him and had not shied away from the journey across the lake to Capernaum. To them, he could now entrust the secret of the true nourishment that gives everlasting life. Christ Jesus himself 'is the Bread of Life that descended from heaven' (Jn 6:50). And by taking up and deepening the experience of the previous day, Christ Jesus can say, 'Yes amen, I tell you, unless you eat of the body of the Son of Man and drink his blood, you will not find life in yourselves' (Jn 6:53).

The development of the Son of Man is made real when the power of faith lives in the human being such that the spiritual can transform the earthly. Through union with the Son of God, who gives us his body and his blood in the sacrament of bread and wine, earthly-natural human beings can transform themselves into Christ-permeated human beings, transforming even their natural being. As Sons of Man, they harbor within themselves deathless, eternal life.

In the subsequent reunion with the disciples, a third path opens for a relationship with the living God and becoming a Son of Man. 'You will see how the Son of Man rises to the place of his true origin' (Jn 6:62).

The first path is the path of spiritually trained knowledge. Nathanael and Nicodemus follow it. The second path is the way of faith, which leads to recognition and action. The two who are healed follow this path. The third path, which the people and the disciples are now shown, is the path of sense perception. The people taste the bread; the disciples 'see' the Son of Man in the Son of God who has become human; the people experience him in their own inner being; the disciples experience him as someone standing before them 'out there.'

Since sensory perception precedes every experience, recognition, and belief, the first path to experiencing the presence of the divine in the earthly world, the path of spiritually trained knowledge, could also be called the first way. Although this path is adequate for our time, yet today we are called upon to keep our senses alert in all areas of life. And is the sensory approach not also the path that art shows us? The manifoldness of art makes us capable of experiencing the diversity of our senses. 'Art,' as Paul Klee writes, 'does not reproduce the visible but makes visible.'* It makes the presence of the divine accessible to us.

'You will see how the Son of Man rises' (Jn 6:62). In the sense just described, sacramental worship, a Christian religious synthesis of the arts, is a path of education, and also for the present human being, a way of perceiving the living God right into the very substances of the earth.

The Greeks turn to Philip on Monday of Holy Week with the request, 'We want to see Jesus' (Jn 12:21). Apparently, they trust their own vision to know whether the one they see is the Messiah. Christ Jesus speaks about a law of the Son of Man. It is the law of dying in order to develop.

> Only when the grain of wheat is laid in the ground and dies does it bear much fruit; if it does not die, it remains unchanged. Anyone who wants to keep his soul unchanged will lose it. But the one who works on their natural soul in this world is building its timeless life. (Jn 12:24f)

Another experience along the path of the Son of Man is given to us. The immortal nature of the Son of Man in us forces us to experience the changes of destiny in life not only as deaths but at the same time as new beginnings for future development and maturation.

* Klee, *Schöpferische Konfession,* pp. 118–22.

❧

Christ Jesus speaks one last time about the Son of Man at the Washing of Feet on Holy Thursday.

> I have performed symbolically what you are to perform out of yourselves, as I did. Amen, the truth I tell you. The servant is no greater than the master, and the messengers no greater than the one who sent them. You are truly great when this knowledge determines your actions. (Jn 13:15–17)

It is not only the striving for our own perfection that is important for us Christians, but especially important is the will to help our fellow Christians along the paths of their spiritual striving. Judas Iscariot, who betrayed Christ, left the circle of disciples.

Jesus Christ's development of the Son of Man is completed through the institution of bread and wine into the body and blood of Christ and the associated founding of the new Christian community.

> Now the Son of Man has been revealed, and God is revealed in him. If God is revealed in him, he will also reveal the Son of Man in himself. (Jn 13:31f)

With this, the future nature of the human being is revealed. Christ Jesus was the first to walk the path towards the unification of God and humanity. Since then, every Christian can also walk towards the goal formulated in the Revelation to John in the words 'I will be their God, and they shall be a son to me' (Rv 21:7).

Jesus Christ is the Son of God in an earthly human being. Through Jesus Christ's earthly life, the seed of a future new order of spiritual beings is planted in the world of God, the hierarchy of the Sons of Man.

10

I Am

Much has been written about John's Gospel and its specific features.* Friedrich Rittelmeyer was probably the first to point out the order and meaning of the seven I AM sayings of Jesus Christ; Christoph Rau also gives a very detailed examination of all the I AM statements found in John's Gospel.†

The purpose of this chapter is to relate the I AM words of Christ Jesus to the experiences that one can have in dealing with one's own I.

We become aware of ourselves in a particular way when we ask ourselves about the intentions of our actions. Why do I act in this way? Am I acting in the heat of the moment? With full conviction? Out of fear? Out of convention? There are countless motives.

The question about ourselves approaches even closer when we become aware of how many things we own and how so little characterises us existentially. What a lot we have! And how little it is if we measure what we are by this abundance.

How fundamentally different, for example, is

---

* For example Rittelmeyer, *Briefe über das Johannes-Evangelium*, Schnackenburg, 'Das Johannes-Evangelium,' in *Herders theologischer Kommentar zum Neuen Testament*, Vol. IV, and Hengel, *Die johanneische Frage: Ein Löungsversuch.*

† Rittelmeyer, *Ich bin*. Rau, *Struktur und Rhythmus im Johannes-Evangelium*, p. 67

10. I AM

our attitude to life when we hear the words, 'I *am* a servant', compared with, 'I *have* a servant'. Our actions are also determined very differently by what we are as a person and by what we have.

But of particular concern to us today, as an expression of our self-determining personality, is acting out of our own responsibility. Our selfhood expresses itself in our accountability. Human beings have been able to acquire this only over the course of cultural history.

A special event along this path took place when Moses (about 1300 BC) and his brother Aaron were tasked with leading the people of Israel out of their captivity in Egypt. In the Old Testament (Ex 3–4), it is reported that while tending the sheep in the desert, Moses is addressed by God out of a thorn bush 'standing with flames.' He receives the commission to lead his people out of bondage. Moses hesitates. 'Who am I, that I should go to Pharaoh and lead the Israelites out of Egypt?' (Ex 3:11). He asks God his name so that he can tell the Israelites when they ask him who is sending him. God says to Moses, 'I AM the I AM; I am the I-will-be. This is what you shall say to the Israelites' (Ex 3:14). Moses is to act out of the divine power of the I-am-I. And when he is to pronounce this name of God before his people, it must sound as if he is speaking by his own authority, even though he is speaking by the divine power of the I-am-I conferred on him.

The creative power of God, which calls into being all that is and will be, his Word, will from now on become effective in human beings through how they take up and carry out their life's mission. This Word of God is called the Logos in the Prologue to John's Gospel.

> In the beginning was the Word, and the Word was with God, and the Word was God. It was in the beginning with God. All things came into being by the same, and except by this, nothing has arisen of what is ... And the Word became flesh and dwelt among us, and we have heard his teaching. (Jn 1:1–3, 14)

The divine Word, which already spoke to Moses and entrusted him with his I-am-I name, became human for the first time in Jesus of Nazareth, and people experienced how spiritual authority and the power of creation emanated from him: 'What is it about his word that full of creative power and strength, he can command unclean spirits so that they flee?' (Lk 4:36). Likewise, people experienced his teaching in the synagogue as an expression of his divine power: 'People were amazed by his words, for he spoke as if God's authority lived in him, and not as the scribes did' (Mk 1:22).

Christ Jesus speaks to the people out of the spiritual power of his divine I. In John's Gospel, he calls himself by the holy name of God: *ehyeh asher ehyeh*, I AM the I AM, the I-will-be. In the Greek text of the Old Testament, this is translated as *egō eimi*.

Christ Jesus spoke to the people about this mystery of his name only in pictures and characterised himself as the bread of life, the light of the world, the door, the shepherd, the resurrection and the life, the way and the truth and the life, the vine (Jn 6:35; 8:12; I0:7; 10:11; 11:25; 14:6; 15:1). Only on rare occasions did he use the shortest, and thus much more effective, form of the I-am-I without an explanatory addition (Jn 4:26; 7:29; 8:23; 14:3).

In addition to these seven I AM words spoken of in pictures, two times the holy name of God is spoken by Christ Jesus as if framing the pictorial I AM words like an arch (Jn 4:26; 18:5).

In the early summer of the year 31, on his way from Judea to Galilee, Christ Jesus comes with his disciples to Samaria, to the well that Jacob once dug. There he meets a Samaritan woman who is drawing water and asks of her, 'Give me to drink' (Jn 4:7). Is the Lord thirsty for the refreshing water of conversation that only human beings can give to each other? Does the woman thirst for the water of perpetual renewal, the knowledge that can only be obtained by turning to the spirit?

The woman is astonished that Christ Jesus, as a Jew, is speaking to a Samaritan woman. In the still warmth of the midday sun, a conversation arises about the sources of earthly and eternal life. In deep trust in the one whom she calls Lord, the woman asks him, 'O Lord, give me such water, that I may not thirst.' His answer is unexpected. 'Go, call your husband, and come back here' (Jn 4:15f). Does this answer indicate that every human being, one-sidedly embodied as a man or a woman, needs the complementary function for the development of their I?

There is a hint of this in the second account of the creation of the human being. He, God, said, 'It is not good that man should be alone; I will give him help, a counterpart' (Gen 2:18). The Samaritan woman has not yet found this complementary counterpart in her life. 'I have no husband' (Jn 4:17); the Lord confirms this. Even after the many men who would have been her counterpart, she now lives with a man who does not fulfill this task. Through these words, the woman feels that she is recognised and confirmed in her deepest being. 'Lord, I feel and see that you are a prophet,' and to the people in the city she says, 'Come out and see a man who has told me everything I have ever done. I wonder if he is the Christ?' (Jn 4:19, 29). Her destiny's deficiency, of which the woman is now aware, opens her eyes to encounter Christ, the Lord of Destiny. Does this mean that only in the polarity of man and woman can our humanity be raised to its divine archetype? This spiritual-divine human being, the I, is neither male nor female. Its most significant ability is to raise the consciousness of the surrounding creation into expression through the word. God speaks and creates the fullness of creation. The human speaks, and the fullness of creation receives individual names. Being a bearer of the Word, the Logos, unites the human with God.

It is against this background that we are to hear the first of the I AM words of Jesus Christ: 'I AM, and I am speaking to you' (Jn 4:26). And the first

10. I AM

of one's own I-experiences is to stand in existence before oneself.

The first of the I AM words that are expressed in pictures makes clear a completely different I-experience. 'I am the bread of life' (Jn 6:35). Bread is a transformed earth substance. One year of work is necessary so that we can eat a piece of bread. Bread characteristically always maintains a self-contained form, whether it be that of a loaf, a slice, a chunk, or a crumb. This is similar to the individuality of the human being, which also shows a distinct characteristic. In this sense, can we see bread as the image of the human I?

When feeding the five thousand, Christ Jesus had taken the five loaves that people carried with them, blessed them, connected his divine nature to them through his Word, and had this new and transformed bread given to the people through the disciples. And thus could each one on the path feel their I strengthened and Christ-ened through the bread.

The next morning, the people met him again with his disciples in Capernaum on the shore of the lake. They had followed him there during the night because they wanted to again be close to the one through whom they had experienced their inner hunger being truly sated.

But unlike the manna the fathers received daily as food from heaven on their journey through the desert, the bread that Christ Jesus gives to human beings is for the inner strength to accept their destiny on earth and to cooperate in the

Christianisation of mortal humanity and a doomed creation (Jn 6:32f).

> I am the bread of life which came down from heaven. Whoever eats of this bread will live in all time. And the bread that I give him is my body, which I give as the life of the world. (Jn 6:51)

The one who strives to live by the divine power of the I AM will not hunger and thirst for gifts from heaven but will strive through their work to transform their natural self into a spiritual human being, into a Son of Man. This addresses the second of the possible I-experiences, love for the earth.

In the autumn of the year 32, during the Feast of Tabernacles, the Pharisees and scribes bring to Christ Jesus a woman they had caught in adultery, a crime punishable by death. They place her in the centre and await his judgment. Through their actions, it becomes clear how dangerous and chaotic the moral feeling and life of humanity is. The light of consciousness, the power of the Logos in it, has become weak, and through the encounter with Christ Jesus is awakened to radiance. As astonishing as it may sound, the Lord calls upon the woman to strive on her path, which until now has proved to be erroneous. The fact that he averts the death sentence speaks of his faithfulness to human beings in all their predicaments. At the same time, he encourages her from now on to seek the right path.

10. I AM

I do not condemn you. Go your way; from now on, sin no more ... I am the light of the world; anyone who walks with me does not walk the ways of darkness. (Jn 8:11–12)

Someone who finds the I in their centre, who affirms themself with all their actions, and faces the encounter with their true self, finds the courage for a new beginning. This is a third I-experience.

The image of the door that Christ Jesus chooses for his I-being speaks of two different abilities of the person who has found their I. We can open ourselves to others and the world, and thus open our inner being to the other. We can also close the door to be by ourselves for reflection and contemplation. Christ Jesus taught this to his own before he gave them the Lord's Prayer. 'When you pray, enter your room and close the door' (Mt 6:6). At the same time, closing the door can also be a sign that we want to close ourselves off from influences that could harm us. The doors of the New Jerusalem are forever open to those whose names are inscribed in the Book of Life (Rv 21:25–27). Yet the gates to the marriage of the Bridegroom in the Kingdom of Heaven will be closed to those who are not prepared (Mt 25:10).

How close these two attitudes of the soul can be becomes apparent in the account that John gives us of the evening of Easter. In devotion to what they have experienced, the disciples are gathered together in the inner room (Jn 20:26).

> When it was late on this first day after the Sabbath, and the doors to the disciples were shut for fear of the Jews, Jesus came and stood in their midst ... A joy that they saw the Lord pulsed through the disciples. (Jn 20:19f)

Gathering oneself within and defending from that which is disturbing, closing the door, leads to an encounter with Christ who is present and alive. The opposite, opening the door to meet him, is described particularly by John in his Revelation: 'Behold, I stand at the door and knock; if anyone hears my voice and opens the door, I will come into them' (Rv 3:20). Before the closed door of the human being's selfhood, Christ pauses and knocks. Each of us knows the knocking signals in our destiny, but it is up to us to hear them and open our inner being so that Christ can enter.

Both are important I-experiences – being open and responsive in the protected inner space and opening up and crossing the threshold to the other.

Another I-experience is connected with Jesus Christ's saying, 'I am the good shepherd' (Jn 10:11). For centuries, God as a shepherd was familiar to the religious feelings of people. The divine kings of Egypt and Mesopotamia, the God of David, Apollo – the sun god of Greece – were all shepherds protecting souls. Now Christ Jesus says it of himself: 'I am the good shepherd.' Does he thereby also open up a view of the self of every human, the divine part of their being? What the Lord says about the characteristics of this I in human beings is groundbreaking. 'The shepherd can be recognised because he enters through the gate' (Jn 10:2). The only legitimate way to reach another person's inner self is to meet them freely and openly.

'He calls each of his sheep by name and leads them out' (Jn 10:3). A true encounter is only possible when I connect with the I of the other person and foster their inner freedom. 'Whoever is a hired servant, his heart is not touched by the fate of the sheep' (Jn 10:13). A life out of the power of the I-am-I is not conceivable without wanting to bear responsibility.

In Bethany, the home of Lazarus, Mary, and Martha, the brother and sisters who are deeply connected with him, Christ Jesus speaks of himself again in the holy I AM form. In the conversation with Martha, who mourns the death of Lazarus, he says to her, 'Your brother will rise from the dead' (Jn 11:23). And when she says she is sure her brother will take part in the resurrection of the dead on the last day of the Earth, a great mystery of the experience of the I AM is revealed in his words. Our I is an eternal being of divine origin:

> I am the resurrection and the life. Anyone who finds confidence in me will find life in death, and every living person who believes in me will not suffer the second death for all time.
> (Jn 11:25f)

But this human I is not to be thought of as a

finished or even static being. According to the will of the Creator, the I is developing and constantly evolving. 'Let us make the human being, a being that is [one day] equal to us' (Gn 1:26). That is, we are to be thought of and experienced as involved in constant development. Goethe calls us a 'characteristic form, living, self-developing', whereby what is unique here is that this development is not brought about from outside but is inherent within this being.*

Is the I also united with its divine Creator through this power and ability? Is the thought of development not only true of the last of his creatures, the human, but also of the Creator God himself? Consider the words spoken by Christ Jesus to the innermost circle of his disciples in the hours of the Last Supper.

> I am the way and the truth and the life. No one comes to the Father except through me. If you had known my nature, you would have known the Father. From now on, you will know him because you have seen him with your eyes. (Jn 14:6)

To walk paths requires inner mobility, and life is not conceivable without development.

With this threefold I AM word, the sphere of experience of the I-am-I expands beyond the certainty of its existential primordial connectedness with God to a view of the goal of becoming the I of every human being who grants Christ space and dwelling within themselves. This is the oneness of the human

---

* Goethe, *Urworte. Orphisch,* tr. Kirk Wetters. *Demonic History,* p. 25: *Geprägte Form, die lebend sich entwickelt.*

10. I AM

and God, of matter and spirit, the revelation of the truth of the unconcealed presence of living spiritual being in sensory appearance. This unity came into being for the first time on earth in Jesus Christ (Jn 1:17).

This goal of humanity, the Christ-development in every human I, is expressed by Christ Jesus in the last of the great I AM words clothed in pictures.

> I am the vine; you are the branches. The one who preserves my being in himself, in him will I work, and he will bring forth rich fruit of the spirit, for without me you will not be able to do anything. (Jn 15:5)

This is community-building in the sign of the I. The image that the Lord chooses for this is eloquent. Almost limitless in its vitality, the vine is united to the earth in its finest branching, penetrating as it were everything. United with the vine, the branches grow. Without it, they are not viable. The inconspicuous blossoms open themselves to the sunlight and to being dusted with pollen. Carried and held by the vine in a fruit cluster, the grapes ripen, each one towards its own perfect development. Their existence is due to the interaction of earth and sky; their vitality comes from the vine. Their community is formed by their individual connection to the same origin.

The first of the seven pictorial I AM words speaks of the mystery of human beings working on themselves in the sign of bread, 'I am the bread of life.' The last I AM word speaks of the mystery of Christian community building in the sign of the vine and its fruit.

Bread and wine are a golden frame in which the stages of the individual's I-experiences are represented in their significance for the community.

The very first I AM word in the Gospel of John is brief; 'I AM, and I am speaking to you' (Jn 4:26). The last word, spoken at the moment of Jesus Christ's arrest, is even shorter. Now it only says 'I AM I' (Jn 18:5). These words affect the soldiers, who, led by Judas, do not act on their initiative, but by order of the Sanhedrin; they lose their balance and fall to the ground. Christ Jesus repeats this I AM statement, adding, 'If you seek me, let them go' (Jn 18:8).

Anyone who lives in the I AM strengthens their courage to shape their life and destiny in harmony with the Lord of Destiny, Christ in them. They do not make anyone dependent on them.

The I-experiences described by the I AM words of Jesus Christ are manifold and exemplary for everyone who seeks such experiences. They are:

- to exist to oneself
- to have love for the earth
- to have the courage to start anew
- to be responsive in one's inner being
- to open oneself to the other
- to bear responsibility

- to seek the revealed truth
- to build community with the help of the I
- to not bind anyone

These create the content of experiences of authentic selfhood.

Thus, the first question, 'What are you seeking?' (Jn 1:38), which the Lord asked those who followed him, can be answered with the words: I am seeking the path of becoming I-am-I in following Jesus Christ.

11

Jesus Christ's Path to the Cross

For about five hundred years, Christians have commemorated the stages of Christ Jesus' journey from Holy Thursday evening, from the Cenacle, the place of the Last Supper on Mount Zion, to Good Friday, the crucifixion on Golgotha and the burial. This path has fourteen stations, and even today, pilgrims still walk it as a processional route in the Holy City.

Countless artists worldwide have tried to depict these stations in pictures, producing wonderful, timeless creations of art.

The first station of the traditional Way of the Cross is Peter's denial of Jesus Christ. He was the spokesman of the circle of disciples, who, in answer to the Lord's question to his disciples, 'Who do you say that I am?' answered, 'You are the Christ, the Son of the living God' (Mk 8:29).

From then on, out of this power of recognition, Peter was promised that the Christian church was founded on him. Now, after the arrest of Jesus, Peter denies him several times with the words, 'I do not know the man' (Mt 26:70–74).

Even if the denial of Jesus Christ by those who are devoted to him is without question a heavy burden for him to bear, we may well be permitted to ask whether it was only then that the Lord's Way of the Cross began. When had he linked his divine destiny to the destiny of mortal humankind, to space and time, life and death, solitude and community, the crosses of our earthly humanity? At his arrest? At the Last Supper? On Palm Sunday or at the descent from the Mount of Transfiguration? Or during the encounter with his adversary, the prince of this world, at his temptation? He said to John before the baptism in the Jordan, 'Let it be done, for it is fitting that we should fully comply with divine justice' (Mt 3:15). Is this the beginning of the Son of God taking on the fate of humankind to redeem us from the soul's sinfulness and death? Is this at the same time the beginning of his way to the cross? To what period of time does he address with the words, 'Since the beginning, you have been united with me' (Jn 15:27)? Did Christ's path to the cross begin with humankind's fall? To deal with these questions in detail would go beyond our scope here, but it is permissible to ask them.

The last station of this Way of the Cross is the burial. But the fundamental statement of Christianity is that the tomb is empty. Certainly, all ways of being born lead to death for us human beings, but Christ Jesus' path leads beyond death to resurrection and the new unity with the Father. Since then, this path has been open for all who connect themselves with him, for he has said:

> In my Father's house, there is room for many.
> If it were not so, would I have said to you that
> I would go to prepare a place for you? And
> when I have gone and prepared a place for
> you, I will come again and receive you into me,
> so that you may be where I am. (Jn 14:2f)

We will not treat all fourteen stations in this account. The intention is to make tangible as an inner sequence of images the path on which Christ Jesus carried the cross of his earthly incarnation to completion on Golgotha

These images can become sources of intense feelings in human souls who seek to inwardly experience and understand the Lord's deeds and sufferings. To follow such a path from event to event helps make us Christ-oriented people.

It is possible to begin with the anointing in the house of the siblings Lazarus, Mary and Martha in Bethany because Christ Jesus speaks there with clear words of his imminent death.

It is the Saturday before Palm Sunday and his triumphal entry to Jerusalem. During the meal, Mary Magdalene takes the most precious oil of the nard and anoints the feet of her beloved Lord and friend. The fragrance of this love permeates the whole house. Christ Jesus rebukes Judas' displeasure at such waste by saying, 'Leave her alone; on the day I pass, what she now does will be fulfilled' (Jn 12:7). The fragrance of a devotional act opens the path towards the completion of Christ's earthly life. Mary Magdalene accompanies him with this attitude until the early morning of the day of his resurrection.

Devotional giving, not expecting anything in return, love for God, is the first step on the path of following Christ.

On the first day of the week of his death, Palm Sunday, his path led him from the quiet privacy of the house at Bethany into the noisy public space of the city of Jerusalem. The people were looking forward

11. JESUS CHRIST'S PATH TO THE CROSS

to the high Passover, expecting the fulfilment of the prophecy:

> Rejoice greatly, Daughter Zion! Shout, Daughter Jerusalem! See, your king comes to you, a righteous helper, gentle and riding on a donkey, on a colt, the foal of a donkey. (Zec 9:9)

And they see it. Coming from the Mount of Olives, Christ Jesus rides into the city on a donkey, among his own. The prophecy is fulfilled.

'Then the whole city was agitated' (Mt 21:10), and the people cried out, 'Praise him! Blessed be he who comes in the name of the Lord, the King of Israel' (Jn 12:13). A shout of rejoicing in a multitude of languages roared around him. Abide, O longed-for and finally-found One! Hosanna to you forever!

Amid the excited crowd, Christ Jesus rides erect and alone towards his self-chosen goal.

He takes animals, old and young, with him on his way. Through human beings, along with all of creation, animals were dragged into mortality; now, they shall have a share in redemption through him.

The image is eloquent: the Lord restores the dignity of the beast, it bears the human being. Who would want to reasonably deny that our earthly body, our 'brother donkey', is similar to the highly developed animal kingdom and that our I, our eternal divine being, needs the supporting help of the body to be active on earth? Palm Sunday is the second stage of Jesus Christ's journey towards the redemption of humanity and the created world through his death and his overcoming of death.

The power of powerlessness fills the soul that submits to the will of God, the Lord of Destiny. Giving up egotistical self-will is the loyalty of the lonely I to itself. To be able to be safely grounded in oneself, to be solitary amid the noisy goings-on of the world, is the second goal on the Christian path of the soul.

How deeply Christ has united himself with human destiny becomes evident in the last hours with his disciples on Holy Thursday evening:

> When Jesus realised that the Father had placed everything in his hands, that he had come from God and was returning to the Father, he rose from the meal, took off his robes, took a cloth, and girded himself with it. Then he poured water into a bowl and began to wash the feet of his disciples and to dry them with the cloth with which he had girded himself. (Jn 13:3–5)

Like a servant who performs the lowest of services, the Lord bends down to the dust of the earth that clings to us human beings; he bows down to the being of each one to give them a new purity. For us Christians, it is not a matter of striving for a spirituality turned away from the earth, but rather of vigilant concrete attention and help for our fellow human beings. 'Since I, your Lord and Teacher, have washed your feet, you also shall wash one another's feet. For I have performed as a sign what you

11. JESUS CHRIST'S PATH TO THE CROSS

yourselves shall perform, just as I did.' (Jn 13:14f). This is the task Christ Jesus gives to all who wish to make an effort to approach his Way of the Cross: the third way-station.

The account of the Last Supper in John's Gospel focuses on Judas' betrayal. Christ Jesus is the first to offer him the bread that was transformed into his body as nourishment for the journey on the night of his self-chosen death. Is this bread for Judas also the pledge of a reunion with his Lord beyond the threshold of death?

Mercy is Christ Jesus' response to the worst that can happen to him through one of his own. It is difficult to bear the cross of betrayal, and a few hours later, it becomes even more burdensome when Peter denies him three times. But we do not hear a word of complaint or even accusation from Jesus Christ.

Is this a task for accompanying the Lord on his way to the Father, to death on the cross? To forgive, to grant mercy to the one who is guilty of wrongdoing, is the fourth way-station on our inner journey.

Up to now, Christ bore the spiritual burdens of betrayal, denial, and service as a servant. The further stations to be mastered are connected with experiences of immeasurable physical pain. Tied to a column, he is subjected to flagellation. He was struck on the chest and shoulders by the blows of the scourge, whose leather straps had fragments of bone and pieces of metal woven into them, which tore rough wounds into the skin. After this torture, the soldiers put him in a purple robe, called him King of the Jews, and placed a crown of thorn branches on his head (Jn 19:1–3). In this way, Christ Jesus is brought before the people to be mocked and ridiculed. He stands upright before the roaring crowd, his head raised to the world of the Father from whom he came, his feet firmly connected to the earth for whose redemption he came, true to his name I AM the I AM, all human, all God.

It is undoubtedly often challenging to affirm life in the body. We know the pain of being bound to our earthly body with its diseases and weaknesses, its demands, the blows of everyday life, exhausted unto death. But would we really wish for a life without pain, the teacher and midwife of new growth and development?

Endurance is an expression of strength, and patience is a virtue to be won on the inner path we as Christians want to walk. We endure scornful laughter of the world that pays homage to the delusion that the human is only a more highly developed animal, as can be seen in its behaviour: exercising the right of the strongest, driven by passions, addicted to the intoxication of power. We nevertheless walk our path, faithful to our origin from God, loyal to ourselves, to the world, to God. Patience and fidelity are not given to us; they are developed.

Christ Jesus continues his Way of the Cross unwaveringly, but he does not walk it alone. Weeping women, members of the Sanhedrin, soldiers, and onlookers, Mary his mother and the disciple whom the Lord loves, all accompany him. On Palm Sunday,

11. JESUS CHRIST'S PATH TO THE CROSS

he included the animal world. On Holy Thursday at the Last Supper, he included the plant world with its representatives of bread and vine. On Good Friday, the One enthroned above all bends down under earthly being, takes along with him the crossbeam, the image of the earth ordained for death. The kingdoms of creation have a share in redemption through him.

Living on this earth as Christians, let us not be inspired by a longing for heaven. We are called upon to transform the earth, and what we want to transform, we must love; otherwise, we will shatter it. Do we not know this in the interpersonal realm? Christ exemplified devotion to his earthly, self-chosen destiny. He demonstrated it in the scourging and crowning with thorns in the sense of the words to his disciples after the washing of feet: 'I have performed as a sign what you yourselves shall perform, just as I did' (Jn 13:15).

Christ Jesus' way to Golgotha is not much further. At that time, the path sloped steeply up from the city. He is nailed to the deadwood of the cross; he is inextricably bound to his creation. The Cross and the Crucified One stand high above it, as if his arms, stretched out, were saying, 'Come to me, all of you who must carry the heavy burden of your destiny' (Mt 11:28). Jesus' hands have become the all-encompassing gesture of love, for 'He carried all that was his in this world to completion in his love' (Jn 13:1).

For countless people, the truth of Good Friday is declared with the Crucified One's words: 'It is accomplished' (Jn 19:30). But suffering, death, and the grave are not the end of Jesus Christ's path. Were it so, Christianity would have no content. The apostle Paul formulates this with all clarity: 'If Christ was not raised from the dead, your faith is an empty delusion' (1Cor 15:14).

The words of the Crucified One himself also point beyond his death: 'Father, into your hands, I commit my spirit' (Lk 23:46). On Good Friday evening, Christ Jesus, the Son of God, the Son of Man, is buried in the grave of the earth. He now embraces the highest heights and the deepest depths. The connection is the cross, the victory banner of our human breed, as Novalis called it.

If we seek Christ Jesus on Holy Saturday, we must follow him into the darkness of death. The Light of the World, Christ, has entered the kingdom of shadows so that light may shine there and the resurrection may prepare itself in the darkness of death.

With the entombment, what the Lord had said to the Greeks in the parable is fulfilled: 'Only when a grain of wheat is buried in the ground and dies will it bear fruit' (Jn 12:24). In the grave of the earth, in the human heart, Christ is sown as seed, to rise and grow.

Along his path of salvation, he took creation with him through death and victory over death; humans, trees, plants, the earth are given new life through him. As Christians we continue this activity in the performance of the sacraments. In bread and wine, in water and oil, in salt and ash, we carry out the holy mystery of transubstantiation through him.

12

An Easter Path

In some places, people go to a decorated spring in the early hours of Easter Sunday, awaiting the rising of the sun. In silence, they light Easter candles and hear the resurrection message from one of the gospels. They sing what is probably the old Christian hymn, 'Christ is Risen,' the original message of Christianity. They then carry home with them the Easter water, an image of the life-giving power of the Christian faith. It is an Easter morning path.

The gospels do not tell us about such a custom, but they do tell us about the journey of the women and of the two disciples Peter and John to the tomb, bringing gifts of offering. The experience of the empty tomb becomes the source of their faith in the resurrection of the Lord.

Christ Jesus had also spoken of himself as a source of eternally living water in quite a different context. This was what happened at the well, in conversation with the Samaritan woman: 'The water that I give to human beings becomes in them a source from which perpetual life issues forth' (Jn 4:14).

For almost two thousand years, this source has been flowing into the world, and we draw from its inexhaustible abundance. The source is his words, as handed down to us in the gospels.

The great conversations are written down especially in John's Gospel, which relates in a particular way to the Creator's Word, the Logos: the conversation with Nicodemus (Jn 3), with the Samaritan woman (Jn 4), again and again with the crowds (Jn 5–10), and with the disciples on Holy Thursday (Jn 14–17).

Unlike the other conversations, the last one, called the Farewell Discourse, is conducted in the calm of farewell:

> Jesus knew that his hour had come in which he should pass from this world to the Father. He carried all that was his in this world to completion in his love. (Jn 13:1)

And thus, he encouraged his disciples:

> Let not your heart become weak. Build on the power that leads you to the Fatherly ground of the world, and that leads you to me. (Jn 14:1)

We are familiar with the gravitas of last encounters, with words spoken and indelibly remembered, or with last letters. Once heard, who does not remember the words and sounds 'For the Last Time,' sung by the choir of knights at Titurel's funeral in Richard Wagner's *Parsifal*?

Jesus Christ's Farewell Discourse, with its crowning in the High Priestly Prayer, has just such an extraordinary power. Spoken in the year 33, the discourse was written down decades later by the disciple whom the Lord loved, who lay at Jesus Christ's bosom at the Last Supper and, lingering on

12. AN EASTER PATH

his heart, asked the question about the traitor. Are these words to be considered a historical document? Yes, they are. They had lived deep inside the beloved disciple, in his memory, until, according to tradition, he wrote them down at a very old age in Ephesus. So deeply had he listened to the essence of Jesus Christ, the Word made human, that his own words were at one with what the Lord had spoken that night in Jerusalem. Through his love, the beloved disciple's memory had itself become divine.

Everyone who entrusts themselves to the flow of this powerful text will notice how this flow carries them, and how the thoughts and words in which the listener is immersed make the original message of Jesus Christ's long speech ever more clear: 'I go to the Father' (Jn 14:12).

When we read or listen to these words, 'I in the Father – you in me – I in you' (Jn 14:20), we are taken along on this journey through death and resurrection to a new uniting of God and humanity.

The Farewell Discourse is a path of the inner experience of the Paschal mystery, expressed in Jesus Christ's words to the disciples, 'I am alive, and you shall raise yourselves into that life' (Jn 14:19).

The disciples were led along this path in Jerusalem that evening by his speaking, and we may discover it by reading and experiencing for ourselves the words of the Farewell Discourse (Jn 14–17).

The Discourse begins with the depth of the Passion experience. The disciples hear their Master speak of his imminent departure: 'Sorrow fills your heart that

I have told you this' (Jn 16:6). They were not able to recognise this parting as the birth of a future human capacity to voluntarily give itself to the God who is alive for all time.

> I will see you again, and your heart will rejoice, and no one can take this joy away from you.
> (Jn 16:22)

To take his words into their hearts was denied to them. Christ Jesus paints a dark picture of their future: 'The prince of this world is approaching' (Jn 14:30). Violence, hatred, and slander will reign:

> ... and the time will come when someone who kills you will think they are doing God a holy service. (Jn 16:2)

But the Lord also reminds them of the power of trust living in their souls since the beginning:

> Let not your heart become weak. Build on the power that leads you to the Fatherly ground of the world, and that leads you to me. (Jn 14:1)

Based on this trust in our union with God as the source of our being, we can find the courage to continue following the path we have begun. Christ Jesus calls it a sin to let this trust atrophy in the soul because this weakness separates us from our divine Father. Using an impressive image from nature, he makes clear to the disciples – to us – where this separation leads:

12. AN EASTER PATH

> Just as the branch cannot bear fruit of its own accord if it does not remain on the vine, so also your eternal being cannot ripen if you do not remain in me. (Jn 15:4)

Christ Jesus is the vine, and Christians live through him and carry his amplified efficacy into the world.

> Anyone who preserves my being within them, in them I will work, and they will yield rich fruit of the spirit for, without me, you can do nothing. (Jn 15:5)

And God the Father, as a wise gardener, watches for healthy development from year to year, from pruning to pruning, and prevents the branches from growing wild.

Those who can keep alive the inner certainty that Christ's love carries us in life and death, even in the night of death and of being alone, through Good Friday and Holy Saturday, can continue on the path to Resurrection on Easter Sunday:

> As the Father carries me in his love, so I build upon your spiritual form with the power of my love ... since the beginning, you have been united with me. (Jn 15:9. 27).

Christ Jesus' love united the circle of disciples and shone over these hours of the Last Supper. This love unites us also today when we Christians offer it to him as love for his church, to which he entrusted the sacraments.

It is through Christ's love for humanity and through the love of Christians for God present in the sacraments that the Christian church is built. For true human communion is formed only through spiritual sharing and not only through social or even financial responsibility.

If this community, formed by the spiritual striving of the individual members, succeeds, then what Christ Jesus has spoken to his own is fulfilled: 'If you keep my spiritual goal alive in you, then you remain faithfully in my love' (Jn 15:10). The spiritual goal, the 'commandment' to which he referred, is the love that respects every human being whose origin is in God, not only every fellow Christian. This love is willing to seek Christ in every person.

With this attitude, the jubilation of Easter can be fulfilled. The words of the Farewell Discourse lead from the deep sadness of abandonment to the joy of meeting Jesus Christ again in all that bears the human countenance.

13
Christ, the Coming One

We are inclined to speak of Christianity as a historical event, acknowledging the words of the New Testament as valid in this linguistic form for all times. At the same time, everyone who seriously endeavours to do so, is aware that such a venerable text came to us from antiquity in Greek. Its translation into our language of today has subjected it to various possibilities of translation and interpretation.

The gospels describe events that took place in a small country two thousand years ago. They established one of the five major world religions and led to a new reckoning of calendar time in the farthest reaches of the earth: before and after the birth of Christ. Nevertheless, it is not the birth of the earthly man Jesus of Nazareth that changes everything, but the human birth of the Son of God, of Christ in Jesus. The earthly life of Christ begins in the thirtieth year of the life of Jesus of Nazareth. With the words, 'You are my Son; today I have chosen you for myself' (Mk 1:11), Mark quotes the Psalm: 'You are my Son, today I have begotten you' (Ps 2:7). With the Crucified One's words, 'It is accomplished' (Jn 19:30), this life as an incarnated human being ends.

For forty days, he appeared to his own as the Risen One in a transformed bodily form (see Chapter 7). Since the Ascension, the words have come to fruition:

'I will not leave you as orphans; I will come to you.' ...
'For a little while longer, and you will no longer see me with your eyes, and then again for a little while, and you will see me ... I will see you again, and your heart will rejoice, and no one can take this joy from you.' (Jn 14:18, 16:16, 22)

In this sense, John's Gospel speaks of Christ not only as one who was but also as the Coming One. And if people are prepared and receptive, his approach is a constantly expanding and renewing event.

From the first to the last chapter, the entire Gospel of John interweaves the motif of coming. The opening chapters speak of Christ's imminent arrival, then of his ever-renewing presence in the human community. The fourteenth chapter onward speaks of his return.

The Logos, the spiritual content of the world, the beginning of everything, is united with God at the beginning of all development, all becoming and is itself divine. It is a light that enlightens humans to the true, unconcealed presence of God in him. This Logos, a synonym for Christ, is *erchomenos,* an ever-present coming of Christ.

꙰

The first for whom his coming is valid are those who are his own. The gospel calls them *idioi*. That could mean that they experience their own being by becoming aware of the fact that they carry within them the image of their origin in God, their immortal I. But these I-human beings closed themselves off from Christ. The danger of egoism is inherent in the I-human. From the very beginning, the threat of rejection accompanies Christ's coming and will remain so. Even before Jesus' birth, it was said, 'There was no room and no shelter for him' (Lk 2:7).

And yet the deepest religious longing of the people awaits the coming of the Messiah, the Anointed One. The Samaritan woman expresses it: 'I know the Messiah is coming, and he will be called Christ' (Jn 4:25). John the Baptist also spoke of the one who will follow him: 'After me comes the one who was before me, for he is my forerunner' (Jn 1:30). In the nocturnal conversation with Christ Jesus, even Nicodemus, a member of the Sanhedrin, speaks of the Messiah's coming as common knowledge in the Sanhedrin. 'Master, we know that you have come to us as a teacher sent by God, for no one would be able to perform the signs of the spirit that you perform if God were not with him' (Jn 3:2).

At a festival in Jerusalem, the Lord himself speaks for the first time of his coming. A dispute arises with the Jews about healing on the Sabbath, which Christ has recently done. He responds to them:

'My Father worked until now; from now on, I also work.'

All the more, the Jews sought to kill him, for he had not only broken the Sabbath commandment, but he had called God his Father and thus made himself equal to God. (Jn 5:17f)

In the course of this first public discussion with the Jews, the question at issue is, by whose authority he acts, and it becomes more and more apparent that the Son can only work in unison with the Father (Jn 5:19, 26, 30, 36 and others). But it is not at all a question of his authority, but instead letting his words become the impetus for one's actions. Not only the knowledge of him that John the Baptist, Nicodemus, and the Samaritan woman had is important; we must connect ourselves existentially with him. In the Farewell Discourse on Holy Thursday evening, he says this with the words, 'You are my friends whenever you take my will into your actions' (Jn 15:14).

This does not happen naturally by itself, nor is it God-given; it can only be a free act of human will. Jesus Christ's pain that this is so difficult may resonate in what he said in the temple in Jerusalem, 'You will not come to me to find life ... In the name of my Father I came, and you will not receive me' (Jn 5:40, 43).

The way Christ speaks about his coming is firmly reinforced when he appears a second time at the

13. CHRIST, THE COMING ONE

Feast of Tabernacles. 'You know me, and you know where I am from. It is not out of myself, however, that I have come; rather, it is the bearer of the truth who has sent me' (Jn 7:28).

His coming into the world causes a new human decisiveness: 'I came into this world for a decision. The eyes of those who do not see shall be opened, and those who think they see shall be blinded' (Jn 9:39).

Through his coming, a new way of seeing will be cultivated in the world. As reported in the creation (Gn 3), human vision had changed through a newly acquired ability to know, the ability to see facts. But now, the incarnation of the Logos, God's incarnation in Jesus of Nazareth through the baptism in the Jordan, gave us the possibility to see the living spiritual essence within the material-earthly. This is what Christ Jesus speaks about with his disciples on Holy Thursday evening, pronouncing the mystery of the new vision:

> 'If you had recognised my being, you would also have recognised the Father. From now on, you will know him, because you have seen him with your eyes'
> Philip asked him, 'Lord, make the Father visible to us; it will be enough for our soul.'
> Jesus replied '... Whoever sees me sees the Father ... I in the Father, the Father in me.'
> (Jn 14:7–11)

This new ability to see, to be able to perceive the living spiritual essence in the earthly-material, probably also prompted the Greeks to turn to Philip on Monday of Holy Week with the request, 'Sir, we want to see Jesus' (Jn 12:21). This request also makes clear that this new ability is not a gift that is given to human beings by nature, but a new capacity to be developed by using one's own will.

This human endeavour of turning to God out of one's free inner self and the power of one's own will corresponds to the will of the Lord, which he associates with his coming:

> All those who came before I worked in human beings are thieves and robbers ... I have come that they may have life, an abundance of life. (Jn 10:8, 10)

The serpent's seduction brought an overabundance of death to human vision. In its place, a new kind of seeing will one day be born that will make Christ perceptible in the kingdom of the living, the kingdom into which he leads humanity. 'I am alive, and you shall raise yourselves to that life' (Jn 14:19).

Again, it is a question of the activity of those who are his. 'You shall raise yourselves,' he says, not 'I will raise you.' Yet we may base our efforts on his help, for he calls himself the good shepherd (Jn 10:11) and characterises the good shepherd with the words:

> He calls each of his sheep by name and leads them out. When he has released all those who belong to him into the open, he goes ahead of them, and the sheep follow him, for they know his voice ...

13. CHRIST, THE COMING ONE

> And I recognise those who belong to me, and they follow me. From my power, they receive timeless life. Nothing can destroy them for all time. (Jn 10:3f, 27f)

These words clearly express the human being's freedom in a relationship with God. Called by their innermost name, they are released into freedom, and it is up to them to determine the direction of their path. If they decide to follow it, to follow the path unwaveringly to the redemption of humanity and creation, they do so as a voluntary act of will. To put one's own will at the service of God's will is an act of supreme human freedom.

Christ Jesus characterises the relationship between human beings and God with the words:

> You are always my friends when you accept my will in your actions. I no longer want to call you servants without responsibility, because the servant does not see what his master is doing. I will call you friends. (Jn 15:14f)

Here, Christ Jesus expresses the goal of his incarnation, of his coming at the turn of time: we are called to cooperate with God in redeeming the world.

But in the Farewell Discourse on Holy Thursday and the report of the Ascension (Ac 1:9–11), there is also talk of a future coming of Christ, his *parousia*, his future dwelling places. 'I will come again and receive you into me, so that you may be where I am.' (Jn 14:3). A little later, Christ Jesus spoke of his imminent return. 'For a little while you will no longer see me with your eyes, and then again for a little while, and you will see me' (Jn 16:16). In the circle of the disciples, the opinion arose that Christ's return was imminent.

In his Letters to the Thessalonians, Paul speaks of this imminent expectation. 'The time has come. He himself, the Lord, will descend from the heights of the spirit, accompanied by an archangel's call and the sound of God's trumpet.' (1Th 4:16). This return will lead to a new connection with the God who lives through all times. 'We live to meet the return of our Lord Jesus Christ, and a new unity with him' (2Th 2:1). And it will be up to us to help him in his power to transform and heal the world:

> He, the God of Peace, consecrates your whole
> being in perfect unity of spirit, soul, and body,
> so that it may be preserved in pure light on
> the day of the return of our Lord Jesus Christ.
> (1Th 5:23)

Through following Jesus Christ, human beings in their tripartite nature as spirit, soul, and body, become the instruments of his redemption, consecrated by God.

Christ's future coming in the clouds (Ac 1:9), the kingdom of the life-forming forces of the earth, finds its preparation in the forty days during which the Risen One is united with his disciples. 'When it was late on this first day after the Sabbath ... Jesus

13. CHRIST, THE COMING ONE

came and stood in their midst and said, "Peace be with you".' (Jn 20:19). The text leaves the reader free to decide whether 'in their midst' is the middle of the room where the disciples are gathered or the centre of every individual who experiences the Lord's greeting of peace.

In the disciples' encounters with the Risen One, his coming is mentioned on several occasions. When meeting with the disciples at the Sea of Galilee, he speaks one last time of his coming. The disciples had laboured in vain the entire night, yet they caught nothing (Jn 21:3). The ability to find nourishment for life at night seems lost. At dawn, they meet the Risen One, who has come to the shore of the lake. At the boundary between firm ground and the fluid play of the waves, they follow his advice: 'Throw out the net at the right hand of the boat, and you will find food' (Jn 21:6).

The catch is exceedingly great, and they recognise their Lord and have a meal with him. After the meal, there is a conversation with Peter about his love for Christ Jesus. Three times the Lord asks him about it.

Three times Peter affirms his love for him. Then Peter turns around and sees John, the beloved disciple, on the same path of discipleship and asks the Lord about John's destiny: 'Lord, what about this one?' (Jn 21:21). And now, in that morning hour on the shore of the Sea of Galilee, in the Risen One's last words recorded by the writer of John's Gospel, he speaks of his future coming. 'If I wish him to remain until I come, what does that mean for you?' (Jn 21:22).

This question is not the Lord's rejection of Peter in the sense of, what business is it of yours? But it is a hint that these two disciples and the soul powers attributed to them, love of duty (Peter) and faithfulness to oneself (John), will be of particular importance for the living God's future work in the world. Together they both prepare the place of the coming God's return in us.

Not only is Christ's coming a historical event. Since his ascension, we have also been living towards his *parousia,* his ever-new presence in every human being who prepares their inner being as his dwelling.

14

Remain in Me and I in You

Like a golden frame, there is a single word that surrounds the Gospel of John from its first to its last chapter. It is the word 'remain' or 'abide'.

The gospel reports how, soon after his baptism near Bethany at the Jordan, Christ met John the Baptist with two of his disciples. One of the two is Andrew, the brother of Simon Peter. The other is unnamed. These two followed Jesus, and when he asked them what they were looking for, they answered with a counter-question, 'Master, where do we find you? Where are you staying?' Christ Jesus' answer is simple. 'Come, and you will see' (Jn 1:38f). Do not remain in your accustomed security. Take the step onto the untrodden path, and you will find and see the living God.

Christ Jesus will only give a real answer to the disciples' question at the end of being with them. 'I remain in you' (Jn 15:4). God is not found in the expansive canopy of heaven, nor in the forces of nature like the God of the Old Testament, but in human beings who prepare their hearts to become his dwelling place.

We hear of few places in his earthly homeland where Christ Jesus stays with the people; a few days in Capernaum (Jn 21:12), two days in Sychar (Shechem of the Old Testament, Jn 4:40), in Galilee

(Jn 7:9), three days in Bethany at the Jordan (Jn 11:6). To outwardly stay for a longer time is not a concern for Christ Jesus.

People's longing for permanence and unity is great. We remember Peter's request on the Mount of the Transfiguration: 'Lord, how beautiful it is for us to linger here. If you want, I will build three huts here' (Mt 17:4). But the Lord leads the disciples down from this elevated experience to where his help is needed for sick humanity (Mt 17:14–18).

Christ Jesus' staying or abiding probably means a different quality than merely staying in one place. This becomes clear for the first time in the conversation he has with the people who followed him on the shore of the Sea of Galilee the morning after feeding the five thousand. They were looking for the continuation of what they had experienced when the Lord had taken the bread they had with them, blessed it and broken it open so that his power would become their food on their way into the night. On that morning, Christ Jesus indicates a food that will remain in people and awaken the timeless life in them. 'The Son of Man will give you this nourishment' (Jn 6:27).

As the conversation continues, it becomes clear that here in Galilee, one year before his Passover death and the institution of the sacrament at the Last Supper, he speaks of himself as the food that creates eternal life in human beings:

> Unless you eat of the body of the Son of Man and drink his blood, you will not find life in yourselves. Whoever eats my body and drinks my blood carries timeless life within, and I

14. REMAIN IN ME AND I IN YOU

> shall rise in them at the end of time. For my body is the true food, and my blood is the true drink. Whoever eats my body and drinks my blood remains in me and I in them.
> (Jn 6:53–56)

Many people who heard him speak in this way were irritated by his words. Even some of his disciples found them unacceptably difficult (Jn 6:60).

> As a result, many of his disciples left him, withdrew, and did not stay with him any longer.
> So Jesus asked the twelve, 'And you, will you also go away?' (Jn 6:66f).

The incarnation mystery of God's Son, the presence of the living God in Jesus of Nazareth, and even in the substances of the earth, is still hidden. The disciples sense it by hearing him speak, and Peter can declare it for all twelve: 'Lord ... the power of your words awakens eternal life. And we have believed and recognised that you are the Holy One of God' (Jn 6:68f). The disciples recognise Christ Jesus as the Messiah by the way he entrusts his word, his being, the lightest of earthly substances, to the air. His breath becomes the bearer of the Logos, the spiritual content of the world. His word to the disciples is also valid for us who are born anew. 'If you are at home in my words, you are my true followers. You will know the truth, and the truth will make you free.' (Jn 8:31f). Hearing the Word and finding our home in his Word makes us Christians.

But his words can become fruitful in us only if we make them our own, if they transform us. This inner process of restructuring what is heard into the certainty of faith needs to be strengthened by the spiritual light that radiates into the world from the living essence of Christ Jesus. 'I have come into this world as the light so that no one who trusts in me will remain in darkness' (Jn 12:46).

Seed placed in the earth does not remain in earth's darkness but, by dying, grows into life with the help of the sunlight. Likewise, God's Word is rooted in the depths of the soul, and with the help of Christ's light of grace grows into the strength of our faith. Christian worship supports this. It awakens, illuminates and inspires all our human senses so that we can perceive the presence of the living God even in the substances of the earth, in bread and wine, in water and oil, in salt and ash. Taking part in sacramental worship fulfils Jesus Christ's words: 'Anyone who walks with me does not walk in darkness, for the light of life will shine upon them' (Jn 8:12).

One year later, on Holy Thursday, Christ Jesus speaks again to the closest circle of disciples about being united with him. He uses the following image:

> Remain faithful in me, and I will remain in you. Just as the branch cannot bear fruit out of its own strength unless it remains on the vine, so can your eternal being not ripen unless you abide in me. (Jn 15:4)

And this picture makes clear that remaining in Christ and his remaining in us is not only the opportunity of every individual who strives to live in Christianity. Beyond that, it is an existential concern of a Christian church to which all belong who feel the healing power of Christ, as the Creed of The Christian Community expresses it. This Christian church is the guardian of the mystery of remaining in Christ through cultivating the holy sacraments entrusted to it.

The church and its members turn towards the world with a double task. They cultivate both devotion and prayer while responsibly shaping everyday social and cultural conditions. Both belong together, and one without the other is neither helpful nor meaningful.

In his final conversation with his disciples at the Sea of Galilee, the Risen One speaks of these two tasks.

After the shared meal, he asks Peter three times if he loves him, and since Peter affirms the questions three times, the Risen Lord points out his duties in the world three times: 'Watch over my lambs, my sheep' (Jn 21:15–17). And when Peter asks about the task of the disciple whom the Lord loved (Jn 21:20), we hear for the last time the word 'remain' from Christ Jesus' mouth: 'If I want that he remain until I come, what does that mean for you?' (Jn 21:22). His answer awakens in Peter – and beyond Peter, in all of us – the awareness that two complementary forces live in the human soul that loves the living God. In the spirit of this last conversation, we can identify them through the two people who are named:

Peter and John. Peter's power says to us, 'Love your obligations and commitments in the world.' The power of John says, 'Be faithful to yourself.' Together, both prepare the lodging in the human soul in which the expected return of Christ can take place.

15

The Human Being: God's Dwelling

Development is appropriate for the Logos. Of all that is, nothing has developed without him. The Creator is to be found in every creature. And yet, creatures have also separated from him, going their own way. Thus they have become counterparts, opposite their Creator.

How do the work and the author relate to one another, the composition to the composer, thought to the activity of thinking, that which has become to that which is developing? Do they readily come together again?

We rightly stand in front of a painting and say, for example, that it is a Picasso. And yet we know precisely that what we have before us is a canvas covered with paint. That we recognise a painter's brushstrokes in these areas of colour and their relationship to one another and then speak of a Picasso is due to our active observation. But the painting itself and its creator have long since separated.

So it is with the Logos and the world created by him. 'Everything has come into being through him, and apart from him, nothing of what was created has come into being' (Jn 1:3). Since the Logos has released everything into existence, creatures have lived in self-ownership. They have become objects apart from their Creator.

The creative Logos contains life within himself, and in human beings, this life becomes the light of consciousness (Jn 1:4). Is it not through thinking that most of what comes into our consciousness through our senses becomes word again? Is not thinking humanity's primal creative activity? And yet it is up to us whether we give our consciousness content with the help of our senses, or whether we drift off to sleep and lose our bright daytime consciousness.

In essence, therefore, thinking human beings are not easily connected with their divine origin. It is up to them whether they want to establish a connection to God the Father and to Christ, the divinely creative Logos, or whether they close themselves off.

The Prologue to the Gospel of John describes this process in detail. The Logos – a synonym for Christ – enters into the human realm, to his own *ta idia*. He becomes human in Jesus of Nazareth, and *hoi idioi*, his own, the people in their free existence, the I-aware humans, did not accept him (Jn 1:11). John's Gospel often speaks of this rejection of God who had become human.

Immediately after speaking of this rejection of Christ, however, it becomes clear that some I-aware humans are devoted to him. 'But those who received him could reveal themselves through him as children of God' (Jn 1:12).

Under certain conditions, then, there is the possibility that the Logos may find reception in humans and may dwell *(eskenōsen)* in them

15. THE HUMAN BEING: GOD'S DWELLING

(Jn 1:14).* This is impressively described, and it is worthwhile to look closely at the two verses, Jn 1:12 and 13.

Verse 12a: *hosoi de elabon auton, edōken autois exousian tekna Theou genesthai.* But those who received him could reveal themselves through him as children of God.

hosoi as many as	Despite an indefinite number in the plural, this is not to be understood as a group, but individually, each one.
de however	Therefore it is not a natural process but, requires the human being's voluntary decision.
elabon accept, receive	It is not a process completed in the past, but rather a process that is continuously being brought to life anew.
auton, him	A very specific someone, who, through receiving, individualises what is received. God can be experienced differently by each human being.
edōken gave	He joins, adds.
autois them	To each in the community.
genesthai to be	The recognition of one's own I in its divine origin.

The second part of the sentence and the subsequent sentence describe the method of how this receiving happens and for what purpose.

---

* The Greek word used here means to erect a tent, a hut. The *skene* in the Greek theatre was the elevated place reserved for the actors, where they spoke from. In the human being, the Logos, Christ, has a prepared place for his activity on earth.

Verse 12b: *tois pisteuousin eis to onoma autou,* who trusted his name

Verse 13: *hoi ouk ex haimatōn, oude ek thelēmatos sarkos, oude ek thelēmatos andros all' ek Theou egennēthēsan,* are born not of blood, nor of the will of the flesh and not of the human will, but of God.

pisteuousin believe	Increasing our recognition to acknowledgment and irrevocable security is a faith activity that gives access.
eis into	into the other person's I-am-I.
to onoma the name	Faith should not be directed towards an image of God, because that carries the danger of defining and delimiting God. The name I AM the I AM also means I am now, and, through the definite article, non-interchangeable, and yet I am different and new in every moment of experience.
ouk ex haimatōn, oude ek thelēmatos sarkos, oude ek thelēmatos andros not from bloodstreams, not from the will of the flesh, not from human will	Not from the blood ties of the family or the people, nor from natural evolution nor human arbitrariness; as it were from below,
all ek theou egennēthēsan but born of God	But born of God from above (as in Jn 3:3)

15. THE HUMAN BEING: GOD'S DWELLING

Faith based in recognition and acknowledgment opens the way for the human being to encounter the God of the I-am-I inwardly, as 'you in me – I in you' (Jn 14:20). This revelation of God within the human I is like a new birth amidst life.

John's Gospel describes this in its reports of individual encounters with Christ Jesus (see Chapter 3).

We hear about Nathanael (Jn 1:45–51), who is prejudiced by his idea that the Messiah could only come from Judea, but not from Nazareth in Galilee. He overcomes his prejudice by seeing and recognising Christ Jesus within his innermost being. He is the first to say it: 'Teacher, you are indeed the Son of God' (Jn 1:49). His openness and testing insight have become faith and knowledge for him.

Christ Jesus' conversation with the Samaritan woman at Jacob's well leads her to a new knowledge of herself. She is seeking the water that gives life, which quenches her thirst forever (Jn 4:14). This leads her to question whether the one with whom she is speaking is indeed the awaited Messiah (Jn 4:29). During the conversation, her request for the water of life expanded and deepened into questioning the right place for worship. The answer she received from the Lord made it clear that in the future, the source of worship will be the human heart.

> O woman, believe me, the time is coming
> when you will not pray to the Father either
> on this mountain or in Jerusalem. The time is

coming, and it has already arrived, when the
true worshippers will pray to the Father in
spirit and in truth; and the Father is waiting
for them. God is spirit. Only those who live in
the spirit and are imbued with truth can pray
to him. (Jn 4:21–24)

Neither mountain heights with their proximity to heaven, nor the venerable sanctuary of the temple in Jerusalem, but the innermost heart of the human being will become the spiritual place for worshipping God.
In his First Letter to the Corinthians, Paul will later refer to this inner place as a temple:

Are you not aware that you are a sanctuary of
God and that the spirit of God wants to dwell
in you? God will punish anyone who harms
the temple of God, for the temple of God is
holy, and you are that temple. (1Cor 3:16f)

This becomes an experience in a very particular way for the man born blind in Jerusalem (Jn 9). After his healing, he realises that the place where he can meet God is within himself. His destiny of being born blind had taught him early on to be sensitive to what was happening within him. Had the healing touch of Christ Jesus and his question, 'Do you believe in the Son of Man?' (Jn 9:35) led him to find the divine I AM within himself? Had his exclusion from the community of those who believed in the Law (Jn 9:34) strengthened this inner power? Besides Christ Jesus, he is the only person who

15. THE HUMAN BEING: GOD'S DWELLING

claims the holy name of God: *egō eimi,* I AM the I AM (see also Chapter 10).

In the figure of the disciple whom the Lord loved, John's Gospel describes most impressively the way a person finds their I through an encounter with Christ (see Chapter 2). Someone who has found their I within themself through encountering Christ Jesus knows that their path as a Christian leads to his side.

Our I can become God's dwelling place on earth in the sense of the words of the first verses of John's Gospel: 'But those who received him could reveal themselves through him as children of God' (Jn 1:12).

For us, the path to becoming God's children is, at the same time, a path towards the founding of the I-am-I within us.

16

Knowledge and Faith

In normal usage, we use the two words *recognise* (or *know*) and *believe* as opposites. Whatever escapes our probing thinking about the world, we must simply believe, whereby the word *simply* then sounds slightly disparaging. Believing is an activity of our mind that eludes any applicable and comprehensible testing method; whereas to recognise or know is an activity of our mind that, with the help of verifiable sensory perception or logic, leads to understandable results in thought.

For example, a person born with healthy visual organs can have their perception of the colour 'blue' checked by any equally healthy person, and they will be able to arrive at the same conclusion. A person with weak colour vision will come to a different conclusion about the same object of perception and can only agree in good faith with tested, joint results because they trust those who report it.

Both activities of our spirit, recognising and knowing as well as believing, have the same goal – encountering beings in the world around us and spiritual beings within us. The starting points of these activities, however, are quite different. In the world, knowledge based on recognition is ignited through our sensory perceptions. Seen from this perspective, a realisation or recognition is always preceded by the activity of one of our senses.

Faith, on the other hand, forms in our heart or our innermost self, as the unmistakable certainty of the truth that we have experienced or worked out for ourselves. Both these activities of our mind belong together, even if they do not penetrate each other. They stimulate and enhance each other.

Perhaps they are comparable to the two great, closed systems in the human organism, the nervous system, and the blood vessel system. They cannot exist without each other but have entirely different functions.

In the disciples' meeting with the Lord at the Sea of Galilee, the writer of John's Gospel now brings together knowledge and faith. There is a long discussion with the crowd, troublesome for both sides, about nourishment from the divine world and about Christ Jesus being the bread of life; many people doubt and separate from him. Even the ranks of the disciples are beginning to thin (Jn 6:66). When asked whether the Twelve are also leaving him, Peter answers the Lord, 'Lord, to whom shall we go? The power of your words awakens eternal life. And we have believed and recognised that you are the Holy One of God' (Jn 6:68f).

In the human being, knowledge and faith are compatible if their respective roles are clearly distinguished.

Both can be learnt, and the writings of the New Testament are a help for us to know Jesus Christ so that our faith in him can be formed and strengthened. In this way, the Lord himself has become our guide to knowledge and belief.

The appearance of John the Baptist and Jesus of Nazareth at that time coincides with people's longing to be able to hear the voice of God again. For centuries, the voice of the prophets had been silent, so the tremendous impact of John the Baptist and his prophetic call, 'Change your hearts and minds, for the kingdom of heaven is at hand' (Mt 3:2) is understandable. 'They came from all the lands around the Dead Sea, from Jerusalem and from the coastal regions of Tyre and Sidon' (Lk 6:17), 'All the people ... understood in their hearts the call of God, and were baptised by John' (Lk 7:29).

Through the emergence of John the Baptist, new hearing and recognition can begin again for people. But even the knowledgeable Nathanael (Jn 1:45f) and Nicodemus (Jn 3:9) meet the new presence of the Lord with scepticism. Even the crowds that hear him speak do not understand his words. 'Why do you not understand my language? Because you are not able to listen to the word of God that goes forth from me' (Jn 8:43). It is not the existence of the organ of hearing alone that is decisive, but the inner attitude with which human beings sharpen their hearing, whether they want to listen. He says, 'Whoever has ears to hear, let them hear' (Lk 8:8) and 'Pay attention to how your listening perceives' (Lk 8:18), that its inner vitality does not atrophy, so that you may be able to hear the word of God.

16. KNOWLEDGE AND FAITH

Two things stand in the way. The first is the unwillingness to recognise and acknowledge what does not belong to the sensory world. This can increase to hatred. 'If you had come from the world, the world would love what belongs to it. But you [the disciples] no longer come from this earth since I chose you for myself out the human world. That is why the world hates you' (Jn 15:19). Preconceived notions dull human cognitive capacity. For example, knowing that the Messiah had to come from Judea meant, therefore, that Jesus of Nazareth could not be the Messiah. Such an inner attitude hinders the ability to recognise and know because it blocks the free view of reality. The consequence is that 'the world cannot receive the spirit of truth [that is, the undisguised appearance of the spiritual in the earthly], because the people of the earth do not see him and do not recognise him' (Jn 14:17). Along with this inability and unwillingness to recognise the spiritual comes the rejection of the spirit, and even worse, its conversion into evil. 'Anyone who is of the spirit hears the spirit revelation of God' (Jn 8:47), the Christ had said to the people, but later they replied, 'Now we can certainly see that a demon is ruling you' (Jn 8:52).

However, since the baptism in the Jordan River, the consolidation of the human and the divine in Jesus Christ had opened up an entirely new possibility for human perception to grasp the divine with human senses.

The sacrifice of the Son of God to become human among men happened in unison with the love of the Father, 'who gave his only-begotten Son ... not that he might judge the world, but that it might experience salvation through him' (Jn 3:16f).

In the Father's love, the Son carries out his redemptive work, because 'the Father has given everything into his hand' (Jn 3:35). In Jesus Christ's words and deeds, in his God-filled teachings and spiritually powerful works, the Father's love is revealed. And so the two are one, which Christ Jesus confirms with the words 'I and the Father are one' (Jn 10:30).

If we want to acquire the life that does not pass away, it is a matter of recognising the essential unity of God, who reveals himself in a triune way, in three different ways. 'For this is the timeless life: that they will recognise you as the only true God' (Jn 17:3).

Knowledge is one path on which we can reach the experience of God in us with the help of our alert senses.

We enter the other path, the path of faith when we learn to observe what the acquired knowledge does in us. Belief does not live in the question, as knowledge does; it arises from confirmation, from inner certainty, from acknowledgment. Belief, faith, has its origin and its support in feeling the secure kinship between the believer and the content of belief, between a person and God's nature and revelation.

Our faith in Christ Jesus and his essential unity with the Father illustrates this. He himself expresses this in the High Priestly Prayer to the Father with the words:

16. KNOWLEDGE AND FAITH

> I have let your essence and your name appear in the people you have entrusted to me from the earthly world. In you, they lived, and you gave them to me, and they carried your word in them ... For the thoughts which you have given me I have given to them; they took them up into themselves and recognised the truth that I have come forth from your being. Their heart is sure that you have sent me. (Jn 17:6, 8)

The very first mention of faith in the Prologue of John's Gospel makes clear what ignites faith and to what goal it leads.

> There was a man sent by God with the name John. He came to bear witness, that he might bear witness to the light, that through it all might believe. (Jn 1:6f)

Does the light that is in human beings, the knowledge of the Logos in them, awaken their faith, or is it the testimony of the one who bears the name of John? The Greek text does not state this clearly. The origin of faith is, therefore, the Logos, the spiritual content of the world. Its goal is characterised in the same textual context: *tekna Theou genesthai, tois pisteuousin eis to onoma autou* 'But those who received him could reveal themselves through him as children of God' (Jn 1:12). The unshakable inner certainty that God is present in the I-am-I makes us certain of our origin in God. Without this faith in the *egō eimi,* human beings are in the greatest danger of their lives, 'for if you do not trust in the true I in me, you will die in your earth-bound state' (Jn 8:24). But if the power of faith lives in them, they will be able to live a deathless life:

> God himself has so turned his love towards the world that he gave his only-begotten Son so that every soul that turns to him in true trust might not perish but rather find timeless life. (Jn 3:16)

After his encounter with Christ Jesus, Lazarus-John had acted out this deep power of trust. His insight had become faith and the starting point of his activities. This power of his innermost self was also the basis of his ability to follow Christ Jesus' call to resurrection.

In this way, the inner certainty of faith in the possible identity of God's I with the human I can also become the source of our actions as Christians in the world. If our human will learns to make the will of God the driving force behind its actions, then 'streams of living water will flow from our bodies' (Jn 7:38). Our certainty of God, our faith, is helpful then not only for us but also for the world around us.

Peter, a spokesperson for the whole circle of disciples, acknowledges Christ Jesus at the Sea of Galilee, saying, 'The power of your words awakens eternal life. And we have believed and recognised that you are the Holy One of God' (Jn 6:68f). Both activities of the human spirit come together in his words. Through the encounter, recognition increases to veneration and acknowledgment and becomes the human power of healing in the world.

We always walk both paths. The more intensively we walk the path of knowledge, the stronger our faith. Just as our physical existence is healthy through the harmonious cooperation of the blood and nervous systems, so is our spiritual existence healthy through the harmonious cooperation of knowledge and faith.

Bibliography

Hengel, Martin, *Die johanneische Frage,* Tübingen 1993.
Herders theologischer Kommentar zum Neuen Testament, Herder 1971.
Kerényi, Karl, *Die Mysterien von Eleusis,* Zurich 1962 (*Eleusis: Archetypal Image of Mother and Daughter,* Princeton 1991).
Klee, Paul, *Schöpferische Konfession,* Cologne 1976.
Kübler-Ross, Elisabeth, *On Life after Death,* Celestial Arts 2004.
Madsen, Jon (trans.) *The New Testament,* Floris Books, Edinburgh 1994.
Moody, Raymond, *Life after Life,* Mockingbird Books 1975.
Ratzinger, Joseph [Pope Benedict XVI], *Jesus von Nazareth,* Freiburg 2007.
Rau, Christoph, *Struktur und Rhythmus im Johannes-Evangelium,* Stuttgart 1972.
Rittelmeyer, Friedrich, *Briefe über das Johannes-Evangelium* Stuttgart 1936.
—, *Ich bin,* Stuttgart 1951.
Steiner, Rudolf, *The Gospel of St John* (CW 103) SteinerBooks, USA 1984.
Varagine, Jacobus de, *The Golden Legend (Legenda Aurea),* Andesite Press 2017. Also available as Kindle book.
Wetters. Kirk, *Demonic History,* Northwester University Press 2014.

You may also be interested in...

The Complete New Testament Studies

Rudolf Frieling

In this collection of essays, Rudolf Frieling draws on his deep knowledge and insight to make the events of the New Testament more understandable to modern readers. He returns to the Greek text to uncover the meaning and power of the original language.

Frieling's masterful analysis surpasses the dry concepts and conventional explanations of many biblical commentaries and brings the events of the New Testament vividly to life. The result is a work that continues to be important for understanding the New Testament today.

florisbooks.co.uk

The Apocalypse of Saint John

Emil Bock

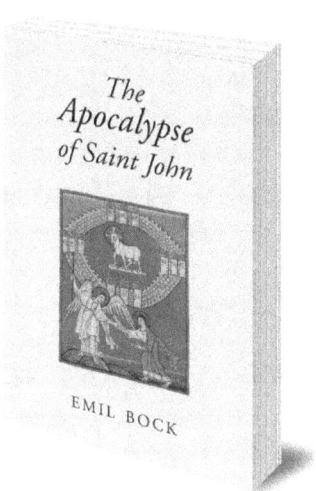

Bock interprets St John's rich pictorial language, often found harsh and mysterious, showing that John is dealing with the universal problems of spiritual development.

This is not just a detailed commentary on the Apocalypse, but a profound and encouraging examination of human needs in today's world. It shows how we can read the Book of Revelation to understand Christ's position as leader through danger in the present and the future.

florisbooks.co.uk

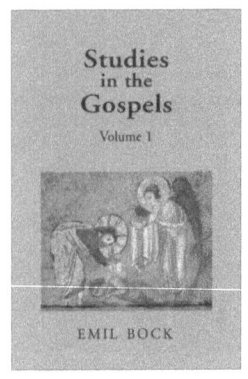  

For news on all our **latest books**, and to receive **exclusive discounts, join** our mailing list at:

florisbooks.co.uk/signup

Plus subscribers get a FREE book with every online order!

We will never pass your details to anyone else.